GRAND CANYON NATIONAL PARK
THE COMPLETE GUIDE

9th Edition

©2023 DESTINATION PRESS & ITS LICENSORS
ISBN: 978-1-940754-51-2

Written, Photographed, & Illustrated by James Kaiser

Special thanks to AJ Lapré, Tom Pittenger, Lon Ayers, Dawn O'Sickey, Colleen Hyde, Pam Frazier, Tricia Lund, Ginger Reeve, Gray Thompson, Cat Zusky, Peter Brewitt, Peter Bohler, Brian Gootee, Clayton Norman, Erin Burgess, Peter Potterfield, Luise Phelps, Jessica H, Karl Kahler, and all the amazing river guides I've met over the years.

As always, special thanks to my family, friends, and all the wonderful people I encountered while working on this guide.

All information in this guide has been exhaustively researched, but names, phone numbers, and other details do change. If you encounter a change or mistake while using this guide, please send an email to changes@jameskaiser.com. Your input will help make future editions of this guide even better. Special thanks to eagle-eyed reader Emma McIntosh for finding a mistake in a previous edition.

GRAND CANYON

NATIONAL PARK

THE COMPLETE GUIDE

9th Edition

WINNER
(First Edition)

Benjamin Franklin Award
Best Full-Color Travel Guide

Independent Publisher Book Award
Best Travel Guide

JAMES KAISER

CONGRATULATIONS!

IF YOU'VE PURCHASED this book, you're going to Grand Canyon. Maybe you're already here. If so, you're at one of the world's most amazing places—an act of geology so massive it can be seen from space, and so beautiful it lures millions of visitors each year.

My first introduction to Grand Canyon was in college, driving cross-country on my way to California. When I reached Grand Canyon, I walked to the rim, basked in the view, and took a few photos. Then I climbed back into my car and headed to Las Vegas. Did I like the view? Of course. Did I realize Grand Canyon had much more to offer? Not really.

A few years later, I realized the magnitude of my mistake. In 2003 I went on my first Grand Canyon river trip. It was one of the most incredible journeys I have ever taken. For three weeks I rafted the Colorado, running rapids and hiking to dozens of spectacular sights—lush side canyons, hidden waterfalls, ancient archaeological ruins. River guides, many of whom spent decades rowing the Colorado, imparted their love and knowledge of Grand Canyon to me. By the end of the trip, I was hooked. I returned again and again, hiking the trails, studying the geology, and learning as much as I could about this amazing place.

Looking back, I can't believe I ever took Grand Canyon for granted. Sadly, many visitors continue to make the same mistake. They step out of their cars, bask in the view, and then run off to their next destination. Vegas? Check. Hoover Dam? Check. Grand Canyon? Check. One of earth's greatest treasures and they missed it!

That's where this book comes in. From hiking to biking to river trips, Grand Canyon has it all. But it's an incredibly overwhelming place. This guide breaks it down, shows you the best Grand Canyon has to offer, and equips you with everything you need to make the most of your time in the park. So go for a hike, drive along the rim, or spend the night at a historic lodge. But whatever you do, don't peek over the rim and wonder what to do next!

CONTENTS

ADVENTURES P.13

Hiking, biking, river rafting, mule riding—Grand Canyon has it all! The only question is what not to do in the park!

BASICS P.116, 248

Everything you need to know, from park fees to seasonal weather patterns. Whatever your plans, arrive prepared to make the most of your time in Grand Canyon.

GEOLOGY P.29

Learn about the powerful forces that shaped Grand Canyon, exposing nearly two billion years of earth history and creating one of the world's greatest natural wonders.

ECOLOGY & WILDLIFE P.41

Far from being a desolate wasteland, Grand Canyon is inhabited by an amazing range of plants and animals. Bighorn sheep, mountain lions, and condors all call the canyon home.

HISTORY P.71

Over the past 10,000 years, Grand Canyon has been home to both prehistoric cultures and modern tribes. First visited by Coronado in 1540, the canyon was avoided by settlers for hundreds of years. In 1869 John Wesley Powell became the first man to run the Colorado River in Grand Canyon—a remarkable adventure that paved the way for further exploration. More recently, Grand Canyon has been center stage for some of America's most historic environmental battles.

SOUTH RIM P.115

The most famous and popular part of Grand Canyon features nearly two dozen breathtaking viewpoints. Spend the night at a historic lodge, bike along the rim, or simply kick back and enjoy the world-class scenery.

NORTH RIM P.247

Wild and remote, the North Rim combines stunning views with just one-tenth the crowds of the South Rim. Because of its cool, high elevation, the North Rim is covered in forests of spruce, fir, and aspen, giving it a feel more like the Rocky Mountains than the desert Southwest.

COLORADO RIVER P.195

Often referred to as the Nile of America, the Colorado River flows free for 277 miles in Grand Canyon. Along the way it passes through a stunning landscape hidden from much of the outside world. A river trip through Grand Canyon is one of the world's most amazing outdoor adventures.

HAVASU CANYON P.283

Part tropical paradise, part Southwestern dreamscape, Havasu Canyon is one of Grand Canyon's most amazing destinations. Home of the Havasupai tribe, Havasu Canyon is famous for the gorgeous turquoise river that tumbles over the canyon's red rocks in a series of stunning waterfalls. The only challenge is getting there.

GRAND CANYON TOP 5

TOP 5 VIEWPOINTS

TOP 5 ADVENTURES

TOP 5 HIKES

TOP 5 WATERFALLS

INTRODUCTION

ONE MILE DEEP. Ten miles wide. Two hundred seventy seven miles long. Covering 1.2 million acres in northern Arizona, Grand Canyon is a breathtaking act of geology. Teddy Roosevelt called it "the one great sight every American should see." The panorama from the rim is one of the most impressive scenes in the world, but Grand Canyon is much more than just a pretty view. Hidden within its depths are geologic marvels, fascinating creatures, the ruins of an ancient civilization, and some of the best outdoor adventures in North America.

Cut by the Colorado River over the past six million years, Grand Canyon is a colossal labyrinth of towering buttes and deep side canyons. The landscape is massive, but most visitors head to one of two developed areas: the South Rim or the North Rim. The South Rim, located two hours north of Phoenix, is by far the more accessible and popular of the two. Home to six of the park's eight lodges, it's what most people think of when they think of Grand Canyon. The North Rim is located just south of the Arizona/Utah border—one of the least densely populated places in the United States. Its remote location means fewer crowds, but with equally stunning views.

Hiking trails descend from both rims to the bottom of Grand Canyon. Along the way they pass through 11 layers of ancient rocks, ranging in age from 250 million to nearly two *billion* years old—almost half the age of the Earth! At the bottom of the canyon, near the junction of three popular trails, lies Phantom Ranch, an overnight lodge that offers comfortable beds and home-cooked meals. Guided mule trips are also offered along several Grand Canyon trails. Both day and overnight trips are available.

Twisting through the bottom of Grand Canyon is the Colorado River. Fed by Rocky Mountain snowmelt before slicing through the deserts of Utah and Arizona, the Colorado is the most impressive river in the West. Although currently plugged by dams along much of its length, the Colorado flows free in Grand Canyon, dropping 2,000 feet in 277 miles. Roughly 25,000 people embark on river trips through Grand Canyon each year. In addition to 60 thrilling rapids, river trips provide access to spectacular hiking trails, stunning archaeological ruins, and gorgeous waterfalls. Without question, a river trip through Grand Canyon is one of the world's most incredible outdoor adventures.

Bright Angel Trail

HIKING

GRAND CANYON OFFERS some of the best hiking in America. The range of scenery is incredible, from cool alpine forests to narrow slot canyons to everything in between. There are trails that skirt the edge of the rim and trails that plunge thousands of feet to the Colorado River. And don't forget Grand Canyon's two billion years of geology—arranged chronologically for your viewing pleasure.

Sound too good to be true? Not at all. But before you hit the trail, there are some important things you need to know. First, there are two types of hikes in Grand Canyon: day hikes and backcountry (overnight) hikes. Day hikes are straightforward—just pick a hike and go. Backcountry hikes require a bit more planning. Due to the large number of visitors interested in backcountry hiking, Grand Canyon National Park limits the total number of backcountry hikers allowed on each trail. This reduces crowding and helps maintain the wilderness experience. Backcountry hikers must apply for permits, which can be a slightly complicated process (p.15).

Unlike most places on earth, many of Grand Canyon's trails start at the top and end at the bottom. This "mountain-in-reverse" style of hiking poses several unique challenges. For starters, a hike into Grand Canyon seems deceptively easy on the way down. Each year park rangers rescue hundreds of hikers who overestimate their ability and become stranded in the depths of the canyon. In general, it takes about twice as long to hike up as it takes to hike down. Another factor is temperature. The lower you go, the hotter it gets, with temperatures up to 20°F hotter at the bottom of the canyon. Despite these challenges, hiking in Grand Canyon is a fantastic experience. Just follow the rules and tips on the following pages for a safe and enjoyable trip.

If you're interested in guided hikes, the Grand Canyon Conservancy Field Institute offers a variety of excellent backpacks, day hikes, and rim walks. The Field Institute, which works in partnership with the National Park Service, is dedicated to enhancing understanding and enjoyment of Grand Canyon through firsthand experience. Many of the trips focus on specific subjects—geology, natural history, archaeology, photography—and many of the instructors are experts in their fields. Field Institute classes accommodate a wide range of ages and abilities. For more information visit grandcanyon.org/classes-tours.

Day Hikes

There are two types of day hikes in Grand Canyon: day hikes along the rim and day hikes that descend partway down the canyon. The North Rim has the best selection of day hikes along the rim, with about half a dozen popular trails. The South Rim has the 12.8-mile Rim Trail, which is mostly paved and passes many popular viewpoints. The South Rim also offers easy access to several trails that can be followed partway down into the canyon. If you plan on day hiking partway into Grand Canyon, know your limits and give yourself plenty of time to return before sundown.

Backcountry Hikes

Grand Canyon offers a number of spectacular backcountry hikes that start at the rim and descend into the canyon. These hikes, best done over multiple days, are called backcountry hikes because they follow trails that pass over terrain classified as "backcountry." The park service divides the backcountry into four management zones: Corridor, Threshold, Primitive, and Wild.

Corridor Zone trails are very well-maintained. There are three in Grand Canyon: the Bright Angel Trail (p.170), South Kaibab Trail (p.180), and North Kaibab Trail (p.276). Not surprisingly, they are the most popular backcountry hikes in the park. Because Corridor Zone trails are heavily trafficked, the park strongly recommends that first-time Grand Canyon backcountry hikers stick to Corridor Zone trails.

Threshold Zone trails are officially unmaintained but generally in fair condition. There are two Threshold Zone trails covered in this book: Hermit Trail (p.186) and Grandview Trail (p.190). The final two management zones, Primitive and Wild, cover extremely rugged terrain beyond the abilities of most Grand Canyon visitors. Considerable Grand Canyon hiking experience is necessary in Primitive and Wild zones.

Grand Canyon's backcountry is also divided into various "use areas." Camping in the popular Corridor, Hermit, Monument, Horseshoe Mesa, and Tapeats use areas is only allowed in designated campsites or campgrounds. Camping in these areas is limited to two nights per campground or campsite per hike. From November 15 to February 28, up to four nights are allowed in Bright Angel, Indian Garden, or Cottonwood campgrounds.

Trail Conditions

Current trail conditions and trail closures are posted on Grand Canyon National Park's website (nps.gov/grca/planyourvisit/trail-closures.htm). It's always a good idea to check current conditions before you hike.

Backcountry Permits

Backcountry permits are required for all overnight hikes. Each year there are roughly 30,000 requests for 13,000 permits. With advance planning and a flexible schedule, however, your odds go way up. The most competitive months are peak hiking season: March through May and September through October.

Backcountry permits cost $10 each, plus $8 per person per night below the rim. Permits are issued by the South Rim Backcountry Office, located behind Maswik Lodge, or the North Rim Backcountry Office, located in the North Rim Administrative Building. Both offices are open 8am–noon and 1–5pm daily.

ADVANCE PERMITS

You can apply for backcountry permits up to four months in advance. A new online reservation system is supposedly in the works. Check Grand Canyon's website (nps.gov/grca) for the latest info. All requests received four months in advance will be entered into a first-round lottery. After first-round permits are processed, permit requests are processed in the order they are received.

LAST MINUTE PERMITS

The park service offers a limited number of last minute backcountry permits. To obtain one, head to the Backcountry Office as soon as you arrive at Grand Canyon and request a number. Numbers are called out the next morning at 8am. If your number isn't called, you will advance up the list for the following day, and the process is repeated. Request a number several days before you'd like to hike and there's a good chance you'll get a last minute permit.

PERMIT TIPS & HACKS

• **Be Flexible**: The backcountry permit application offers an "Additional Choices" section. Fill it out completely and check as many boxes as possible. The more options you give the park, the more likely you'll get a permit.

• **Arrive Early**: Let's say you're part of a group looking for last-minute hiking permits on a weekend during peak season. As long as one person in your group arrives several days early, he or she can climb the last-minute permit list until obtaining one. If you reach the top of the list before the hike, you can swap the top number for a new top number each day until you're ready for the permit.

• **Be Social**: Most backcountry permits are good for up to six people. If you're a small group, and you meet another small group at the backcountry office looking for the same last-minute permit, and they're higher on the list than you, launch a charm offensive and propose joining their permit.

• **Rim to Rim**: The hardest permit to obtain for a Rim to Rim hike is Cottonwood Campground on the North Kaibab Trail. The North Rim Backcountry Office has priority for Cottonwood Campground, so if you're looking for a last-minute permit, you'll want to go there. It's very difficult to get a last-minute Cottonwood permit from the South Rim Backcountry Office.

Hiking Tips

DON'T HIKE TO THE COLORADO RIVER AND BACK IN A SINGLE DAY

Each year the park service rescues hundreds of day hikers stranded in Grand Canyon. Hiking into the canyon is deceptively easy on the way down. By the time exhausted hikers realize how difficult the hike up will be, it's often too late. Evacuations are time consuming and costly. Helicopter evacuations can cost stranded hikers thousand of dollars per flight. Plan ahead, understand the trail, and you can avoid an unnecessary evacuation.

BRING PLENTY OF WATER

The biggest dangers are not scorpions, rattlesnakes, or mountain lions. In fact, these animals pose relatively little threat. The biggest dangers are dehydration, heat exhaustion, and heat stroke. Rangers recommend drinking one gallon of water per day in the summer. Drink small amounts often, even if you don't feel thirsty. By the time you feel thirsty, you're already dehydrated. Some trails have access to water, but many do not. Ask about a trail's water availability before you start hiking. And be sure to filter or purify all water from springs or creeks.

USE EXTREME CAUTION WHEN HIKING IN THE SUMMER

In the sweltering summer months, heat-related dangers are even more pronounced. Temperatures rise as you descend into the canyon. Average temperatures at the bottom of the canyon are roughly 20°F higher than average temperatures along the rim. Try to avoid hiking during the middle of the day, and drink plenty of water.

MAKE WAY FOR MULES

Mules have the right of way on all trails. If you encounter mules, step off the trail on the uphill side. Follow any instructions from the mule wrangler.

BRING PLENTY OF FOOD

Just as important as drinking is eating. Salty snacks replace electrolytes that the body loses through sweating. If you drink water but don't replace electrolytes, you run the risk of developing hyponatremia, which can lead to seizures and death. When hiking in Grand Canyon, eat more than you normally do and eat small amounts often. Adding electrolyte powder to your water is also a good idea.

CHECK BACKCOUNTRY CONDITIONS ONLINE

Grand Canyon's website (nps.gov/grca) has a "Backcountry Updates and Closures" page that lists current backcountry conditions.

FLASH FLOODS & DEBRIS FLOWS

FLASH FLOODS ARE one of Grand Canyon's greatest dangers. During monsoon season from July through early September, thunderstorms sweep through northern Arizona on an almost daily basis. Some storms dump several inches of rain in just a few hours, and the rocky, sun-baked landscape does little to absorb the water or slow it down. Runoff channels into narrow side canyons, forming flash floods that can reach speeds topping 23 feet per second. The floods move so fast they often compress the air in front, sending pebbles and rocks flying through the air. If you find yourself in the path of a flash flood, climb as high as possible as quickly as possible.

Perhaps most frightening, flash floods can form when skies are clear and sunny overhead. Storms near Grand Canyon are often highly localized. They can dump several inches of rain over a concentrated area, while just a few miles away the weather is sunny and clear. In the late summer of 1997, 12 tourists were hiking through Antelope Canyon, just east of Grand Canyon, when a thunderstorm ten miles distant dumped 1.5 inches of rain in less than an hour. The runoff gathered with astonishing speed, sending an 11-foot wall of water roaring through Antelope Canyon. All but one of the hikers was killed. The sole survivor was pressed against the canyon wall, gasping for air as the flood raged past. By the time the water subsided he was completely naked. The muddy, gritty water ripped off every stitch of clothing on his body. Only his boots remained attached to his feet.

Similar to flash floods, but even more destructive, are debris flows. Unlike flash floods, which are 80–90 percent water, debris flows are a deadly slurry of water, rocks, and debris—up to 60 percent solid material by volume. Roaring through side canyons at speeds up to 25 feet per second (three feet per second *faster* than flash floods), debris flows rip out trees and wash away boulders that weigh hundreds of tons. On average, two debris flows are triggered in Grand Canyon each year. Although few people have witnessed a debris flow, the resulting vibration shakes the ground for miles.

MULE RIDES

For OVER A century, mule rides have been one of Grand Canyon's most famous adventures. Everyone from Teddy Roosevelt to the Brady Bunch has ridden mules in Grand Canyon, and while hardcore hikers would never dream of passing up a chance to hike into the canyon, for many people mules are the only way to go. These sure-footed animals offer a genuine taste of the Old West—and they do most of the hard work for you.

Although less demanding than hiking, mule riding is still a physical activity. Riders must sit up straight on a moving animal for extended periods of time, which requires more endurance than you might think. There's also the fear factor. Mules often walk terrifyingly close to the edge of the trail. At times it seems like they're doing this intentionally, taunting you with their amazing sense of balance. Mules have a better view of their hooves than horses, which is why they are used in Grand Canyon. That said, mule riding is not for the faint of heart. Despite a few mild challenges, however, most people have no problems riding mules, and many consider the experience to be great fun.

The South Rim offers both day and overnight mule rides. Day rides head east of Yaki Point along the East Rim Trail. Overnight rides follow the Bright Angel Trail to the bottom of Grand Canyon, where riders spend the night at Phantom Ranch (p.179). Riders return the next morning via the South Kaibab Trail. Two-night rides are also available.

Reservations for South Rim mule rides are accepted up to a year in advance, and they are highly recommended during the busy summer months. The North Rim offers only day rides, including rides along the rim and trips that descend partway down the North Kaibab Trail.

No experience is necessary for mule rides, but riders must be at least nine years old, 4 feet 9 inches tall (1.44 meters), speak fluent English so the mule can understand commands, and weigh less than 225 pounds (102 kg) for day rides along the South Rim and less than 200 pounds (91 kg) for overnight rides to Phantom Ranch.

South Rim Mule Rides: (p.123)
North Rim Mule Rides: (p.251)

COLORADO RIVER TRIPS

A RIVER TRIP through Grand Canyon is one of the world's most amazing adventures. Venture down the Colorado River and you'll be treated to wild rapids, sandy beaches, stunning side canyons, and some of the most breathtaking scenery in North America. The view from the rim is incredible, but the view from the river is beyond belief.

Over a dozen commercial outfitters are licensed to offer guided river trips through Grand Canyon. Overnight trips generally range in length from seven to 18 days, and cost around $300 to $350 per person per day. The best trips are the multi-day adventures run between Lees Ferry (river mile 0) and Diamond Creek (river mile 226). One- to three-day "sampler" trips run at either end of Grand Canyon don't compare to the scenery found in the heart of the park. Some companies offer trips geared to specific interests such as hiking, photography, or natural history. But due to the immense popularity of river trips and the limited number of passengers the National Park Service allows on the river each year, many trips are booked a year or more in advance.

Commercial outfitters run trips with both motorized and non-motorized boats. Motorized boats speed through the canyon, allowing you to see more in less time. While some people find this convenient, others dislike the whirlwind pace. Non-motorized boats come in two varieties: inflatable rafts and dories. Inflatable rafts cushion the impact of the rapids, resulting in a smoother ride. Rigid dories, piloted by skilled guides, offer a more tumultuous ride where flipping is slightly more likely. But flipping is relatively rare, and for many thrill seekers these elegant dories are the only way to go.

Grand Canyon's river-running season generally lasts from mid-April through early November. Summer is the most popular season, but in my opinion it's the worst time to go due to heavy crowds and scorching temperatures. The best time for a river trip is spring or fall, when temperatures are mild and the river is less crowded. Private, noncommercial river trips are also allowed. Private permits are granted by lottery each year.

For more on running the Colorado River through Grand Canyon, see the Colorado River chapter (p.195).

River Outfitters

These outfitters are officially authorized to offer river trips through Grand Canyon National Park. Trips last 3–18 days, and they are offered in rafts, dories, or J-Rigs depending on the company.

Aramark-Wilderness River Adventures
(800-992-8022, riveradventures.com)

Arizona Raft Adventures
(800-786-7238, azraft.com)

Arizona River Runners
(800-477-7238, raftarizona.com)

Canyon Explorations/Expeditions
(800-654-0723, canyonexplorations.com)

Canyoneers
(800-525-0924, canyoneers.com)

Colorado River and Trail Expeditions
(800-253-7328, crateinc.com)

Grand Canyon Expeditions Company
(800-544-2691, gcex.com)

Grand Canyon Whitewater
(800-343-3121, grandcanyonwhitewater.com)

Hatch River Expeditions
(800-856-8966, hatchriverexpeditions.com)

O.A.R.S./Grand Canyon Dories
(800-346-6277, oars.com)

Outdoors Unlimited
(800-637-7238, outdoorsunlimited.com)

Tour West
(800-453-9107, twriver.com)

Western River Expeditions
(866-904-1160, westernriver.com)

CHOOSE YOUR
VESSEL

INFLATABLE RAFT

Oar-powered rafts offer a great mix of safety and excitement. Their flexibility allows them to bounce off obstacles and absorb much of a rapid's energy, resulting in a smoother ride. Tipping is rarely a problem, but expect to get wet. Some outfitters allow passengers to help paddle rafts.

DORY

These sturdy boats require the most skill to maneuver, and they provide the most thrilling ride in Grand Canyon. Made of wood or fiberglass, dories ride like a roller coaster, and they are more prone to flipping over than rafts. But for romantics, purists, and adrenaline junkies, these boats are the only way to go.

J-RIG

These large, motorized rafts are the fastest, most stable craft on the river. Carrying up to 20 people, they transport the majority of commercial passengers through Grand Canyon. Although J-Rigs visit more places in less time than non-motorized craft, some people prefer viewing one of earth's greatest natural wonders at a slower pace.

BIKING

BIKING IS ONE of the best ways to experience Grand Canyon. While other visitors are searching for parking or waiting in long shuttle lines, you'll be cruising along the rim. You'll enjoy the same spectacular views—but at your pace and with plenty of fresh air. What's not to love?

The South Rim has Grand Canyon's best biking. There are over 15 miles of Greenway Trails (paved roads specifically for biking) connecting points of interest around Grand Canyon Village. Bicyclists also enjoy privileged access to 7-mile Hermit Road (p.140), home to some of the South Rim's most popular viewpoints, but closed to private vehicles from March to November. There's even a beautiful three-mile Greenway Trail near the western end of Hermit Road. For those who'd rather avoid Grand Canyon traffic altogether, you can park in Tusayan (p.108) and ride a 6.6-mile Greenway Trail into the park.

Bright Angel Bicycles (928-679-0992, bikegrandcanyon.com) rents bicycles next to the Grand Canyon Visitor Center. Hourly ($12.50), half-day ($31.50), full-day ($42) and multi-day ($36.50) rentals are available. They also offer guided tours. The popular Hermit Road Tour ($48.50–$67.50 per person) shuttles you past Hermit Road's uphill section for a leisurely 5.5-mile ride from Hopi Point to Hermits Rest, where a return shuttle awaits.

The South Rim's free shuttle buses have bicycle racks, so you can bike one-way and catch a shuttle back. Just be aware that each shuttle accommodates no more than three bikes. If you're biking with four or more people, logistics can get complicated. Also note that *you* are responsible for putting your bike on the shuttle rack, which can be a bit confusing. Practice on the dummy bike rack at Bright Angel Bicycles before trying to operate a shuttle rack in the wild.

Biking on the North Rim offers fewer canyon views, and the viewpoints, though gorgeous, are spaced much farther apart. The majority of North Rim roads pass through forest rather than along the rim. (If you visit in autumn, however, you'll enjoy spectacular foliage.) An alternative to paved roads is the Arizona Trail, a 12-mile trail through the forest that's open to bicycles. The best North Rim biking, however, is the Rainbow Rim Trail, located in Kaibab National Forest just outside the park. Over 22 miles of singletrack trace Grand Canyon's rim, passing dramatic viewpoints and great campsites along the way.

Grand Canyon Astronomy

With elevations above 7,000 feet, dry desert air, and minimal light pollution, Grand Canyon has some of the best stargazing in America. If you're not looking up at night, you're missing half the show. Don't know much about astronomy? Inquire about Grand Canyon's free ranger astronomy programs. Or visit in June, when the park hosts the week-long Grand Canyon Star Party, featuring fascinating astronomy talks during the day and dozens of telescopes on both rims at night. The Flagstaff Star Party (flagstaffstarparty.org) takes place each fall, and Flagstaff's Lowell Observatory (p.103) is open year-round.

In 2019 Grand Canyon was certified an International Dark Sky Park by the International Dark Sky Association (darksky.org) after changing thousands of outdoor light fixtures to reduce light pollution. Today nearly two-thirds of Americans live in cities and towns with so much light pollution they can no longer see the Milky Way. But here in Grand Canyon the Milky Way, which reveals the heart of our 200-billion-star galaxy, still blazes across the sky each night.

Long before modern astronomy, native tribes developed rich mythologies to explain the cosmos. The Hopi believe the Milky Way shows the path of Good People, with a short side branch showing the path of Bad People. Many constellations are named after local wildlife (jackrabbit, bighorn sheep, coyote), and their motion across the sky guides annual cycles of planting and harvesting. The Navajo believe *Náhookǫs Bikǫ'*, the North Star, represents the central fire at the center of every *hogan* (home). On opposite sides of *Náhookǫs Bikǫ'* lie the male guardian *Náhookǫs Bi'ka'* (the Big Dipper) and the female guardian *Náhookǫs Bi'áád* (Cassiopeia), which both revolve around the fire. When *Dilyéhé* (the Pleiades) falls below the western horizon in early May, the Navajo know it is time to plant corn. Stars without names are said to have been scattered by Coyote, the Trickster, who grabbed a pouch filled with crystal star seeds and flung them into the heavens to create chaos. The Hopi call the Pleiades *Chööchökam*, Harmonious Stars That Cling Together, and they are symbolic of the seven universes (three that the Hopi have already passed through, the current universe, and three yet to come). The Southern Paiute believe the Pleiades is a family of seven Paiutes who fled to the sky after a dispute with their father, *Tu-rei-ris*. When *Tu-rei-ris* saw them in the sky, he grew enraged and turned them into *pootsis* (stars). The family retaliated by turning *Tu-rei-ris* into a coyote. Even today, when you hear a coyote howling at the stars, you are listening to *Tu-rei-ris* mourning his lost family.

National Canyon

GEOLOGY

GRAND CANYON IS a geological wonderland. There are few locations on earth with so many eye-popping rock formations on display in a single place. Had they been located elsewhere, many of Grand Canyon's individual rock formations would be world-famous landmarks on their own. But within the depths of the canyon they occur by the dozen. Rainbow-splashed mesas, temples, and buttes cascade down from the rim, extending for miles in all directions. Visually, there is so much to see—so many colors, textures, and shadows—that your sense of perspective melts away. The scope of the scenery is dizzying, which is what makes gazing into Grand Canyon so much fun.

Even if you know nothing about geology, Grand Canyon is still an impressive sight. But take the time to learn about the forces that created it, and you'll look upon the canyon with a fresh set of eyes. What was once amazing will become astounding. What once took your breath away will make your head spin.

On a human timescale, Grand Canyon seems ancient, peaceful, and serene. On a geologic timescale, however, it is young, violent, and exciting. Geologists were shocked to discover that Grand Canyon formed in just six million years. When you consider that earth is over four *billion* years old, six million years seems like the blink of an eye. It's as if northern Arizona suddenly cracked open and—*bam!*—there was Grand Canyon.

In reality, northern Arizona was sliced open by the Colorado River. After tumbling down from the Rocky Mountains, the Colorado twists and turns through the desert Southwest, picking up enormous amounts of sediment along the way. This sediment—a mixture of gravel, silt, and clay eroded from the region's soft rocks—scrapes along the bottom of the river like sandpaper. During massive floods, when 100-ton boulders tumble like ice cubes, the rate of erosion accelerates exponentially. On average, the river has cut downward at a rate of roughly 6.5 inches every 1,000 years.

Over the past six million years, the Colorado has sliced through northern Arizona like a knife through a wedding cake. In the process, it has exposed dozens of layers of progressively older rocks. This gives Grand Canyon one of its defining characteristics: it's one of the few places on earth where you can view nearly two billion years of earth history simply by glancing up and down.

ANCIENT ROCKS

MOST ROCKS IN Grand Canyon are sedimentary rocks, which form when sediments such as sand, silt, or mud gather in thick layers that, over time, transform into rock. Grand Canyon's sedimentary rock layers accumulated over millions of years on the surface of northern Arizona, which has been home to giant sand dunes, muddy river deltas, and shallow tropical seas. These prehistoric environments formed as ancient continents drifted across the globe. As tectonic plates shifted, ancient oceans advanced and retreated over northern Arizona. Eventually, eroded sediments from these prehistoric environments formed distinct layers of sedimentary rocks. Sand dunes cemented into sandstone, mud compressed into shale, and the discarded shells of marine animals cemented together into limestone.

Because Grand Canyon's rocks were laid down chronologically, one on top of another, they reflect a geological relationship known as *superposition*. Simply put, superposition means that rocks above are younger than rocks below. Move your eyes from the rim to the river and you are essentially traveling back into time. At the bottom of Grand Canyon you'll find the region's oldest exposed rocks: Vishnu Schist and Zoroaster Granite. These rocks, referred to as the Precambrian rocks of the Inner Gorge, are the only common rocks in Grand Canyon that are not sedimentary. Vishnu Schist is a metamorphic rock that formed roughly 1.7 billion years ago when intense heat and pressure transformed previously formed shale into schist. About 200 million years later, magma shot up through cracks in the schist and cooled into beautiful veins of pink Zoroaster Granite.

It wasn't until about 550 million years ago that Tapeats Sandstone, the oldest major sedimentary rock in Grand Canyon, started to form. What happened in the one billion years between the formation of Vishnu Schist and Tapeats Sandstone is a bit of a mystery. During that time, up to 12,000 feet of additional rocks formed on top of Vishnu Schist. But by 570 million years ago those additional rocks had eroded away, leaving an enormous gap in the geologic record. Geologists refer to such a gap as an *unconformity*. In Grand Canyon, the gap between Vishnu Schist and Tapeats Sandstone is known as the Great Unconformity—a name given by early explorer John Wesley Powell. After the formation of Tapeats Sandstone, additional sedimentary rock layers continued to accumulate. The youngest sedimentary rock in Grand Canyon is 260 million year-old Kaibab Limestone, which is familiar to anyone who has walked along the South Rim or North Rim.

Another rock formation found in Grand Canyon is the Grand Canyon Supergroup. These rocks started out as sedimentary rocks around one billion years ago, but they were later metamorphosed by heat and pressure. Today rocks from the Grand Canyon Supergroup are visible from only a handful of locations in Grand Canyon, such as Lipan Point (p.164) on the South Rim.

"The thought grew in my mind that the canyons of this region would be a Book of Revelations in the rock-leaved Bible of geology. The thought fructified and I determined to read the book."

—John Wesley Powell

ROCK LAYERS

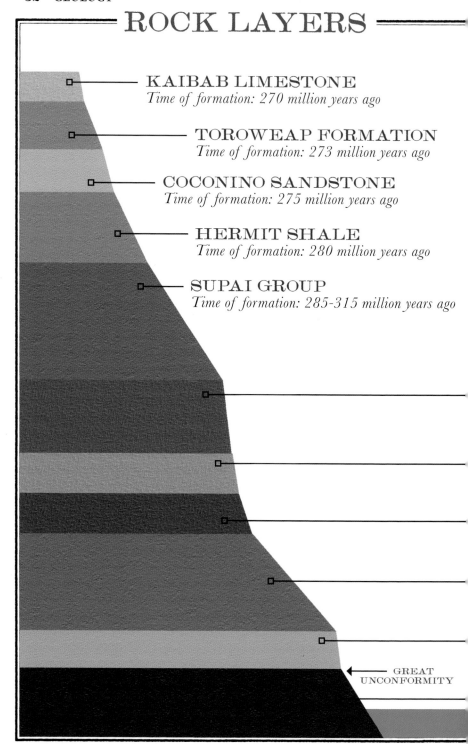

KAIBAB LIMESTONE
Time of formation: 270 million years ago

TOROWEAP FORMATION
Time of formation: 273 million years ago

COCONINO SANDSTONE
Time of formation: 275 million years ago

HERMIT SHALE
Time of formation: 280 million years ago

SUPAI GROUP
Time of formation: 285-315 million years ago

GREAT
UNCONFORMITY

Ancient Landscapes Revealed

Grand Canyon's 11 major rock layers offer a rare glimpse into the ancient landscapes of northern Arizona, which bore little resemblance to the landscape we know today. Roughly 340 million years ago, the region lay under a shallow tropical sea similar to today's Caribbean. Over thousands of years, the shells of dead sea creatures piled up on the seafloor, and over time they compressed into Redwall Limestone. Although limestone is normally white, Redwall Limestone is stained red by minerals seeping down from the Supai Group above. The rocks of the Supai Group formed about 300 million years ago, when eroded debris from the ancestral Appalachian Mountains washed over northern Arizona. (At the time the Appalachian Mountains were over 30,000 feet high, similar to today's Himalayas.) About 35 million years later, northern Arizona was home to a vast desert similar to today's Sahara. Giant sand dunes covered the desert, and over time they compressed into Coconino Sandstone. Today you can still make out the slopes of sand dunes in parts of the Coconino Sandstone, as well as fossilized reptile tracks.

REDWALL LIMESTONE
Time of formation: 340 million years ago

TEMPLE BUTTE LIMESTONE
Time of formation: 385 million years ago

MUAV LIMESTONE
Time of formation: 505 million years ago

BRIGHT ANGEL SHALE
Time of formation: 515 million years ago

TAPEATS SANDSTONE
Time of formation: 525 million years ago

VISHNU SCHIST
Time of formation: 1.7–1.8 billion years ago

THE COLORADO PLATEAU

THE SEDIMENTS THAT formed the sedimentary rocks in Grand Canyon generally accumulated near sea level. So how did they end up thousands of feet *above* sea level? The answer has to do with Grand Canyon's location on the southwestern edge of a huge area known as the Colorado Plateau. At 130,000 square miles, the Colorado Plateau is the second largest plateau in the world after the Tibetan Plateau. It covers much of the Four Corners region, and it's filled with some of the most stunning scenery in America.

Starting around 60 million years ago, forces deep within earth began pushing up the Colorado Plateau. By about five million years ago, the Colorado Plateau had risen over a vertical mile. The higher elevation led to increased precipitation, which led to increased erosion that stripped away many of the region's rocks. During this time, several thousand feet of overlying rocks were removed above Kaibab Limestone, which caps the top of Grand Canyon today.

As erosion slowly chipped away at the Colorado Plateau, it sculpted one of the most dramatic landscapes in the world. Aside from the physical beauty of the sedimentary rocks, the rock layers are notable because they are so exquisitely preserved. This is due to the relative stability (geologically speaking) of the Colorado Plateau. Over the past 600 million years, as continents drifted across the globe, they smashed into one another like bumper cars, twisting and deforming their landscapes. But the Colorado Plateau was sheltered from much of this action. As a result, its sedimentary layers remain relatively intact. By contrast, the rock layers in the geologically active regions surrounding the Colorado Plateau, such as the Great Basin and Rocky Mountains, have been severely deformed.

Some geologists believe the Colorado Plateau resisted deformation because the earth's crust is relatively thick in the Four Corners region. In places, the crust beneath the Colorado Plateau is up to 25 miles thick. The crust of the Great Basin Desert, by comparison, is only 16 miles thick. So rather than buckle and break as it pushed upward, the Colorado Plateau remained relatively unaltered as a single tectonic block.

The uplift of the Colorado Plateau continues today. By some estimates, it has risen as much as 1,000 feet over the past one million years. During this time, there have been some notable catastrophes along its boundaries. In western

Grand Canyon, which lies near the boundary of the Colorado Plateau and the Great Basin, the earth's crust is thinner and more broken. As a result, hundreds of volcanoes have erupted over the past two million years. At least 150 eruptions have sent lava pouring over the rim of Grand Canyon. After tumbling down to the Colorado River, the lava cooled and formed massive dams that often backed up the river for miles. The largest dam, called Prospect Dam, was over 2,300 feet high—three times higher than present-day Hoover Dam. It created a massive reservoir that took 22 years to fill and stretched hundreds of miles to present-day Moab, Utah. In as little as 20,000 years, however, the gritty Colorado River completely eroded Prospect Dam.

THE COLORADO RIVER

MORE THAN ANYTHING, the Colorado River is responsible for the creation of Grand Canyon. But that's only part of the story. The specifics are considerably more complex. Early geologists, starting with John Wesley Powell, assumed the modern river has always followed its present course. The way they envisioned it, the river cut down into northern Arizona as the Colorado Plateau rose up around it.

Then, in the 1930s and '40s, geologists came to the startling conclusion that the Colorado River has not always followed its present course. Although the ancestral Colorado River did flow into northern Arizona, passing through the region that would one day become eastern Grand Canyon, it avoided western Grand Canyon entirely. Rather than flow west through Arizona, the river flowed north into Utah.

This led to a frustrating dilemma. If the ancestral Colorado River avoided western Grand Canyon entirely, how did western Grand Canyon form? That question has yet to be answered definitively. Unfortunately, much of the evidence has eroded away, so facts are hard to come by. But geologists have pieced together a general theory.

Back when the ancestral Colorado River flowed north into Utah, a second "lower" Colorado River originated somewhere west of Grand Canyon. Over time, the headwaters of the lower Colorado River eroded east until they reached the western edge of the Colorado Plateau. As they continued to carve away at the landscape, the headwaters came closer and closer to the upper Colorado. Around five million years ago, a critical divide was breached between the two rivers. The lower Colorado captured the upper Colorado, and the upper Colorado began flowing west. At that moment, the modern Colorado River was born.

For the next five million years, the modern Colorado River sliced into the landscape as the Colorado Plateau rose up around it—pretty much the way early geologists envisioned it. But the river's rate of downward cutting has not been constant. The rate of erosion varied considerably depending on which rocks the river cut through. Soft sedimentary rocks (such as sandstone and shale) were cut through relatively quickly. Harder sedimentary rocks (such as limestone) took much longer.

Despite varying rates of erosion, the Colorado River cut through all of the sedimentary rocks in a remarkably short period of time. By about 3.8 million years ago, Grand Canyon was within 500 feet of its current depth. At that point the river was in contact with Vishnu Schist, the hardest rock in Grand Canyon, and its rate of downward cutting significantly slowed. Meanwhile, another characteristic of the river started to change. As the Colorado River ground down steep obstacles that once choked the river, its grade began to level out. Rivers with gentle grades are much less erosive than rivers with steep grades, so the Colorado's rate of downward cutting slowed. Over the past one million years, the river has cut down less than 50 feet.

This shocking fact reveals a tremendous amount about the creation of Grand Canyon. While the Colorado sliced into northern Arizona like a band saw between three million and five million years ago, it has done relatively little since then. Erosion in Grand Canyon does not occur at a steady rate. Rather, it happens in brief spurts when powerful forces pound away at the landscape. Periods of intense erosion almost always correspond to periods when massive obstacles—lava dams, the uplift of the Colorado Plateau—block an easy path for the river. The Colorado River doesn't just find the path of least resistance. It creates it. This gives one pause when considering the fate of the man-made dams that hold back the river today.

THE CANYON GROWS

ALTHOUGH THE COLORADO River is remarkably good at cutting down, it barely makes a dent horizontally. In fact, the river often *adds* inches to the riverbank by depositing sediment. Yet in places Grand Canyon is over ten miles wide. What's going on?

Although the Colorado River carved a remarkably deep channel, the width of Grand Canyon is mostly due to runoff from the rim. In both cases the mechanics are similar—gritty water grinds down the region's soft rocks, breaking them into sediment that's eventually flushed out of the canyon. As runoff from Grand Canyon's rim flows down to the Colorado River, it erodes the canyon's steep walls. In effect, the Colorado River's deep channel serves as a giant template, funneling much of the surrounding runoff into the canyon.

The rate of erosion, however, varies considerably from rim to rim. The walls of the North Rim have eroded up to *ten times* faster than the walls of the South Rim. This has nothing to do with the rocks being eroded—both rims share the same rocks—but rather the amount of precipitation that tumbles down from each rim. Both sides of Grand Canyon are tilted slightly south. As a result, precipitation that falls on the North Rim runs *into* Grand Canyon, while precipitation that falls on the South Rim runs *away* from Grand Canyon. Because the North Rim receives significantly more runoff, its walls erode at a much faster rate—a fact apparent to anyone who has visited both rims. Viewed from the South Rim, the walls of the North Rim gradually recede into the distance. Viewed from the North Rim, the South Rim's cliffs seem like a nearly vertical wall.

Despite their varying slopes, both rims cascade down to the Colorado River in stairstep formation. This pattern is also due to variable rates of erosion. Just as the Colorado River cut down through Grand Canyon's rocks at different rates, the same rocks eroded horizontally at different rates. Soft rocks erode easily to form gentle slopes, while hard rocks resist erosion to form steep cliffs. Stairstep rock layers are one of the defining characteristics of Grand Canyon. To experienced hikers the cliffs and slopes are like trail markers, constantly reminding them of their relative depth in the canyon.

Grand Canyon is filled with deep side canyons, which often form along faults. The faults create narrow channels that gather runoff, and over thousands of years the runoff carves deep side canyons. The larger the side canyon, the more runoff that gathers, accelerating erosion in a self-reinforcing process.

Flowing water causes most erosion in Grand Canyon, but other forces are also at work. Frost wedging occurs when water freezes and expands in the cracks of rocks, producing massive pressures—up to 20,000 pounds per square inch—that can split the rocks apart. In some cases, frost wedging triggers rockfalls that send massive chunks of rock tumbling down the canyon. Rockfalls also occur when soft rocks erode beneath hard rocks, creating an overhang that eventually collapses under its own weight. This process is called *slab failure*. In Grand Canyon, with its many alternate layers of hard and soft rocks, slab failure is common. It's also the reason why so many of Grand Canyon's hard rock layers erode to form steep cliffs.

In short, an extraordinary combination of factors led to the creation of Grand Canyon. Tectonic forces, rock formation, and erosion all conspired to create the stunning landscape currently on display. Millions of years from now, those same powerful forces will have rendered Grand Canyon unrecognizable to modern eyes. So consider yourself lucky. You're alive for that brief moment (geologically speaking) when you can enjoy one of earth's most amazing creations.

Want to learn more about geology? Visit the Yavapai Geology Museum (p.128) or attend a ranger Geology Talk.

Clarence Dutton

Many geologists have written about Grand Canyon, but few have done so as articulately and eloquently as Clarence Dutton. His 1882 masterpiece, *Tertiary History of the Grand Cañon District*, metamorphosed dry geological investigation into compelling, lyrical prose. In 1874 Dutton was 33 and living in Washington, D.C., when his quick mind caught the attention of John Wesley Powell. The famed explorer recruited Dutton to map the largely unexplored region Powell called the Colorado Plateau. The stark geography was unlike anything Dutton had seen on the East Coast. It made "the heart ache and the throat tighten." Dutton named many of Grand Canyon's most prominent features after gods from ancient religions: Vishnu Temple, Isis Temple, Buddha Temple, Vulcans Throne. His dramatic writing was accompanied by realistic illustrations by William Henry Holmes—a bold departure from the dull scientific descriptions and exaggerated illustrations that previously depicted the region. He declared Grand Canyon "the sublimest thing on earth. It is so not alone by virtue of its magnitudes, but by the virtue of the whole … its intricate plan, the nobility of its architecture, its colossal buttes, its wealth of ornamentation, the splendor of its colors, and its wonderful atmosphere. All of these attributes combine with infinite complexity to produce a whole which at first bewilders and at length overpowers."

"The Grand Cañon at the Foot of the Toroweap"
William Henry Holmes

Blooming Agave

ECOLOGY

MORE SUBTLE THAN Grand Canyon's geology, but equally fascinating, is the park's ecology. Visitors sometimes assume Grand Canyon is barren and lifeless. This is anything but the case. Over 6,000 feet of sudden elevation change creates a wide range range of life zones lying remarkably close to one another. Nowhere is this more apparent than the North Kaibab Trail, which starts in cool boreal forests on the North Rim and ends in scorching desert at the bottom of Grand Canyon. In a matter of hours, hikers pass by spruce trees and cacti—the equivalent of traveling from Canada to Mexico in a single day.

All told, Grand Canyon is home to 17 fish species, 48 reptile species, 91 mammal species, and over 440 bird species. There are also over 1,700 plant species in Grand Canyon—more than any other national park.

This impressive biodiversity is due, more than anything, to temperature and precipitation, both of which are affected by elevation. In general, temperatures rise and aridity increases as you descend into Grand Canyon. From rim to river, the environmental contrast is often extreme. At the bottom of western Grand Canyon, an average of six inches of rain falls a year, and only rugged desert plants like cacti and yucca can survive. The cool, high plateaus of the North Rim, meanwhile, often receive over 30 inches of precipitation a year, supporting dense forests of spruce, fir, and aspen.

Grand Canyon's wide range of climates also affects the distribution of animals. Cold-blooded reptiles thrive near the bottom of Grand Canyon, but they are much less common on the rim. Animals that thrive on the rim often require a steady source of water, so they are poorly suited to the dry depths of Grand Canyon. The distribution of animals is also affected by the distribution of plants, which form the foundation of a healthy food chain.

Plants are also dependent on animals. Consider the relationship between pinyon pines and pinyon jays, pale blue birds found throughout the Colorado Plateau. Pinyon pines produce large seeds that are too heavy to be dispersed by wind. But the seeds are a staple of the pinyon jay's diet. After gathering pinyon seeds, pinyon jays bury them for later use. Some seed caches are forgotten, however, and those seeds often grow into new trees. Pinyon pines provide jays with an important food, and pinyon jays ensure a healthy population and distribution of pinyon pines.

When viewed as a whole, plants and animals found in particular areas form unique, interdependent communities called "biotic communities." From tropical rainforests to Arctic tundra, biotic communities exist around the world. In Grand Canyon there are six major biotic communities: boreal forests, ponderosa forests, pinyon-juniper woodland, desert scrub, and the lush riparian habitat on the banks of the Colorado River. These biotic communities generally form horizontal bands across Grand Canyon.

Because elevation has such a strong effect on temperature and climate, it seems logical that the location of biotic communities could be based on elevation alone. Although elevation does provide a rough approximation, many local environmental factors also come into play. One example is microclimates: small pockets of temperature and moisture that vary dramatically from their immediate surroundings. Microclimates are caused by a variety of environmental factors including local topography, proximity to water, and exposure to sunlight. South-facing slopes receive much more sunlight than north-facing slopes, making them significantly warmer and drier, even at higher elevations. This explains why desert plants such as yucca are found at high elevations on the south-facing North Rim, while shady pockets on the South Rim support small populations of Douglas fir, an alpine tree that generally avoids the South Rim's warmer, drier climate.

Air currents also affect microclimates. During the day, as the sun heats the ground, hot air rises from the depths of Grand Canyon. At night, by contrast,

C. HART MERRIAM

The concept of biotic communities, or "life zones," where specific plants and animals interact, was first developed at Grand Canyon by the biologist C. Hart Merriam. In 1889 Merriam, then director of the U.S. Biological Survey, led an expedition to Grand Canyon to study the region's plants and animals. As he descended into the canyon, he noticed distinct communities of plants and animals living together. He called these communities "life zones" and theorized that their location was due to varying temperatures. Additional research revealed that life zones are dependent on much more than just temperature. But Merriam's Grand Canyon expedition was the first time plants and animals had been studied living together in a quantifiable way. His groundbreaking work helped pave the way for the modern study of ecology.

GRAND CANYON WEATHER

Because Grand Canyon is located in the arid Southwest, it receives much less precipitation than most parts of the country. The precipitation that does fall arrives in a fairly predictable pattern, falling in winter and summer in a nearly 50/50 split.

In summer, prevailing winds from the south carry moisture from the Gulf of California. As moist air passes over Arizona, it's lifted up and over the highlands just south of Grand Canyon, arriving at the South Rim cool and condensed. In the morning, as the sun heats the inner canyon, hot air rises and collides with the cool, moist air above. This sudden collision creates short-lived afternoon thunderstorms. In July, August, and early September, a period referred to as "monsoon season," these storms dump rain on Grand Canyon nearly every afternoon.

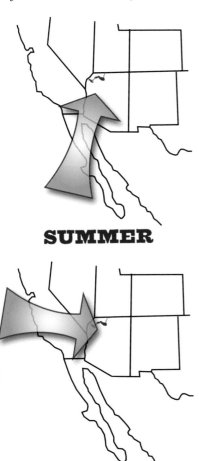

SUMMER

WINTER

In winter, prevailing winds from the west and northwest carry moist air from the Pacific Ocean. Most of this moisture is wrung out by the Sierra Nevada Mountains, but some finds its way into northern Arizona. Although winter storms in Grand Canyon are much less intense than summer storms, they often linger for days.

In spring and fall, Grand Canyon is extremely arid, resulting in dramatic temperature swings. Dry air allows up to 90 percent of solar radiation to reach the ground during the day. At night, however, the situation is reversed. Up to 90 percent of Grand Canyon's accumulated heat radiates back into the atmosphere through clear, dry skies. In humid areas, by contrast, just 40 percent of solar radiation reaches the ground during the day, and that heat is often reflected back by an insulating cloud cover at night.

ICE AGE
in
Grand Canyon

Twenty thousand years ago, near the peak of the last Ice Age, Grand Canyon was a very different place. Although the topography was nearly identical, the distribution of plants and animals would have been unrecognizable to modern eyes. In the depths of the Ice Age, a cool, wet climate descended over the Southwest, forcing many plants and animals to lower, warmer elevations. Juniper trees, which currently grow on the South Rim, grew along the banks of the Colorado River, and Douglas fir, a tree currently found only at the park's highest elevations, grew on the Tonto Platform, 3,000 feet below the rim.

Many strange and wonderful creatures roamed Grand Canyon during this time, including mammoths, camels, and Merriam's teratorn, a 50-pound bird with a wingspan more than *12 feet* across. Grand Canyon was also home to the Shasta ground sloth, which was roughly the size of a grizzly bear and weighed over 500 pounds. Around 15,000 years ago, however, many of these large Ice Age animals went extinct, most likely due to the arrival of a new predator in North America: humans.

As the glaciers that covered much of North America retreated between 15,000 and 10,000 years ago, the Ice Age drew to a close. In the Southwest, temperatures rose, the climate dried out, and plants and animals living in Grand Canyon migrated towards the rim. By about 8,500 years ago the inner canyon had been transformed from woodland to desert. The remarkable flexibility of Grand Canyon's plants and animals—retreating to the warm inner canyon when temperatures drop, climbing to the rim when temperatures rise—is a powerful reminder that the park's seemingly fixed life zones are, in fact, highly dynamic cool air flows down from the rim. These invisible rivers of air, flowing up and down Grand Canyon, allow a wide range of plants to survive in unlikely places.

Because biotic communities are packed tightly together in Grand Canyon, their boundaries often blur. In fact, many plants and animals live in multiple biotic communities. But even though Grand Canyon's topography often brings unlikely plants and animals together, it can also act as a barrier. Consider Abert's squirrels, small grayish squirrels that are dependent on ponderosa pines as a source of food. During the Ice Age, when the climate was much cooler and wetter, ponderosa forests grew in the depths of Grand Canyon. For thousands of years, Abert's squirrels roamed these ponderosa forests. But around 10,000 years ago, when global temperatures started to rise, ponderosa pines migrated to higher, cooler elevations—and with them went the Abert's squirrels. Some squirrels went to Grand Canyon's South Rim and others went to the North Rim, creating two distinct Abert's squirrel populations. Over time, Abert's squirrels living on the North Rim developed unique physical characteristics, most notably a striking white tail, that led scientists to classify them as an entirely separate subspecies: the Kaibab squirrel.

The interaction between plants, animals, and landscapes is complex in any environment. But in Grand Canyon—one of the most rugged and dynamic environments in the world—that interaction is even more complex. Even seasoned naturalists find themselves struggling to comprehend the sophisticated ecology of the park. But that's what makes Grand Canyon so fascinating. There's always something new to learn about Grand Canyon's amazing plants and animals, which is what keeps many nature lovers coming back year after year.

Grand Canyon Caves

Grand Canyon has thousands of caves—more than any other national park—but only a fraction of those caves have been explored. Some that have been explored contain the remains of extinct Ice Age animals. In Rampart Cave, located in western Grand Canyon, archaeologists discovered the remains of Shasta ground sloths, including bones, skin, and hair. The cave even contained fossilized sloth dung, which was 20 feet deep in places. Although Grand Canyon's massive, inhospitable terrain hinders extensive exploration, the arid environment is ideal for the long-term preservation of bones and animal remains. With so many caves still unexplored, who knows what other discoveries lie waiting in the depths of Grand Canyon?

Shasta ground sloth skull

HUMAN CHANGES

THE ARRIVAL OF humans in North America roughly 15,000 years ago coincided with the extinction of many large Ice Age mammals such as horses, camels, and sloths that once roamed Grand Canyon. Whether these extinctions were due to over-hunting or the arrival of previously unknown diseases remains a mystery. Following the extinctions, however, Grand Canyon's distribution of plants and animals remained relatively stable for thousands of years. But in recent years the park has experienced many subtle—and not so subtle—changes.

The most notable change has been to the Colorado River. For thousands of years, the Colorado flowed free above Grand Canyon. Melting snow in the Rocky Mountains unleashed annual spring floods, but by winter the Colorado's volume shrank to a fraction of its peak. The temperature of the silty water also varied dramatically throughout the year. Over tens of thousands of years, a handful of fish evolved to survive in these unusual conditions. Eight fish species are native to Grand Canyon, and six of those species live only in the Colorado River Basin.

In 1963 Glen Canyon Dam plugged the Colorado River upstream of Grand Canyon. Almost overnight, the river's downstream ecology completely changed. Instead of spring floods and winter trickles, the river now had a consistent, steady flow. And because dam-released water was drawn from the dark, chilly depths of Lake Powell, it entered Grand Canyon frigid and silt-free. The cold, clear water provided terrific habitat for over a dozen non-native fish, including trout, which were introduced for sportfishing. But the arrival of non-native fish has been disastrous for native species. Non-natives compete with natives for food, and some new species actively prey on native fish. Since the construction of Glen Canyon Dam, three native fish species have disappeared from Grand Canyon and two, the humpback chub and razorback sucker, are struggling to survive.

The humpback chub, which first appeared three to five million years ago, evolved in swift, muddy waters. As a result, it has some remarkable biological adaptations. Large fins allow it to easily maneuver rapids, and small eyes protect it from silt. Perhaps most interesting, when swift water passes over its pronounced hump, the chub is forced down toward the bottom of the river where the current is less strong. This helps humpback chub stay put during floods. Humpback chub

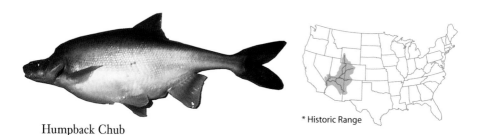

Humpback Chub

* Historic Range

thrived in the virgin Colorado, but their population plummeted after the completion of Glen Canyon Dam. Although they can survive in cold, dam-released water, they need warm water to spawn. In 1967 humpback chub were declared an endangered species, and today only a few thousand survive in Grand Canyon. Most live at the confluence of the Colorado River and the free-flowing Little Colorado River.

In 2009 the National Park Service began relocating juvenile humpback chub from the Little Colorado River to Shinumo Creek, a small tributary of the Colorado further downstream. A waterfall in Shinumo Creek prevents non-native species from entering the creek's upper reaches, providing safe haven for young humpback chub. The establishment of a satellite population of humpback chub is critical for the long-term success of the species. A hazardous materials spill in the Little Colorado River, for example, might otherwise prove disastrous.

Glen Canyon Dam also dramatically affected the banks of the Colorado River in Grand Canyon. Massive spring floods once roared through Grand Canyon, scouring the riverbank and preventing many plants from taking root. Over the past several decades, however, the dam's steady, consistent releases have eliminated large floods, and a dense thicket of shrubs and trees has sprouted along the riverbank.

One of the new arrivals is tamarisk (aka salt cedar), a plant native to the Middle East that was brought to North America for erosion control in the late 1800s. Tamarisk is remarkably resilient, and it spread like wildfire along rivers throughout the Southwest, arriving in Grand Canyon in the 1920s. Following the construction of Glen Canyon Dam, tamarisk became the dominant plant species along the Colorado River in Grand Canyon, muscling out native plants that provide important habitat for native species. (Tamarisk does, however, provide valuable nesting habitat for the southwestern willow flycatcher, which is listed as an endangered species.) The National Park Service began cutting down tamarisk in 2000, and since then hundreds of thousands of plants have been removed from Grand Canyon. In 2001 the tamarisk leaf beetle, a non-native insect that feeds on tamarisk, was intentionally released in the West, and by 2009 it had reached Grand Canyon.

Non-native species have also affected Grand Canyon's vast rocky spaces. When miners abandoned their search for riches in Grand Canyon in the late 1800s, they often left pack animals behind. Burros, which are originally from the deserts of Africa, were rugged enough to survive on their own. By the 1970s there were as many as 350 feral burros living in Grand Canyon. Because the burros competed with bighorn sheep for scarce resources, they were rounded up and transported out of Grand Canyon by helicopter. Many feral burro populations remain throughout the Southwest, however, and there are occasional reports of feral burros in western Grand Canyon.

Mountain Lions & KAIBAB DEER

Uncle Jim Owens

In 1906 President Theodore Roosevelt established Grand Canyon Game Reserve on the forested Kaibab Plateau just north of Grand Canyon. James Owens, who became known as "Uncle Jim," was appointed manager of the reserve, and from 1906 to 1918 he shot more than 600 mountain lions. The walls of his cabin were covered with mountain lion claws, and a sign outside advertised, "Lions Caught to Order, Reasonable Rates." At the time, mountain lions were considered vicious "varmints" with an insatiable appetite for wild deer and domestic cattle. Exterminating such ruthless predators was considered both logical and necessary.

Between 1906 and 1924, however, the number of deer on the Kaibab Plateau exploded from 4,000 to 100,000. The deer population soon outstripped the available food supply, and over the next two years roughly 60,000 deer died of starvation. Biologists concluded that the rapid rise and fall of the deer population was caused by the systematic reduction of mountain lions, which preyed upon deer and kept their population in check. The "Kaibab Deer Incident" became a fixture in biology textbooks, demonstrating how man's interference with nature can upset its delicate balance. It was referenced in both Aldo Leopold's *A Sand Country Almanac* and Rachel Carson's *Silent Spring*, two of the most influential environmental books of the 20th century.

Then, in 1970, biologist Graeme Caughley challenged the basic assumptions of the Kaibab Deer Incident. He questioned the deer population data, which was determined largely through guesswork, and concluded that mountain lions played a relatively small role in regulating the deer population. Caughley argued that habitat changes caused by climate, ranching, and government policy had a far greater impact on the deer population than mountain lions. His conclusions gained wide acceptance, and references to the Kaibab Deer Incident were removed from many textbooks.

In recent years, however, Caughley's study has been challenged by biologists who believe that mountain lions did, in fact, play a significant role in regulating the Kaibab deer population. The Kaibab deer debate, it seems, is far from over. Perhaps the real lesson is that the natural world is often far more dynamic and complex than it appears at first glance. Despite all we have learned, our scientific understanding of nature is far from complete, and there is much that remains to be discovered.

Gooseberryleaf Globemallow
Sphaeralcea grossulariifolia

Mojave Aster
Xylorhiza tortifolio

Palmer's Penstemon
Penstemon palmeri

Cardinal Monkeyflower
Mimulus cardinalis

Desert Four O'Clock
Mirabilis multiflora

Mariposa Lily
Calochortus flexuosus

Prince's Plume
Stanleya pinnata

Grizzly Bear Prickly Pear
Opuntia polyacantha

Evening Primrose
Oenothera pallida

Brown-Spined Prickly Pear
Opuntia phaeacantha

Desert Columbine
Aquilegia desertorum

Silverleaf Nightshade
Solanum elaeagnifolium

Utah Agave
Agave utahensis

Utah agave is one of three agave species found in Grand Canyon, along with Parry agave and Schott agave. Also called century plants, agave are famous for their giant flower stems, which shoot up after several years and measure up to 12 feet. One famous agave species, the blue agave, is used to make tequila in Mexico. Despite its name, Utah agave is found in only a tiny sliver of southwest Utah. Most of its range is in northeast Arizona and southern Nevada, where it has been an important food for thousands of years. Native tribes place agave hearts in roasting pits with hot coals, cover the pit with dirt, and allow the tough plant to cook for several days. When removed, the heart is soft and sweet, with a flavor somewhere between a sweet potato and a pineapple. There are hundreds of agave roasting pits in Grand Canyon, including one near Three-Mile Resthouse on the Bright Angel Trail. That roasting pit, which is over 2,500 years old, was built on Redwall Limestone, which retains more heat than other rocks. Because the roasting pit is located near the edge of a cliff, ashes and debris could easily be raked out and discarded.

Banana Yucca
Yucca baccata

These spiky plants are easily identified by sharp, dagger-like leaves that grow up to two feet long. In spring a tall stalk filled with creamy white flowers rises from the center of the plant. Banana yucca, named for its banana-shaped fruit, is one of half a dozen yucca species in Grand Canyon. Although sometimes misidentified as cacti, yucca are actually giant members of the lily family. Well-adapted to arid environments, their curved leaves help channel rainwater and dew towards their roots. Yucca were among the most useful and important plants for Grand Canyon's native tribes. Women wove the plant's strong fibers into ropes, baskets, mats, and sandals. Yucca fruit was eaten, and yucca root was diced and put in water to make soap and shampoo.

Sacred Datura
Datura wrightii

These dazzling white flowers grow on
sandy roadsides throughout the Southwest.
The petals, which can grow up to eight inches long,
close into a tight cylinder on hot, sunny days to reduce
evaporation and conserve water. When temperatures
drop around dusk, the petals unfurl into one of the largest
flowers in Arizona. Hawk moths with a proboscis (tongue) up to a
foot long drink datura nectar and pollinate the trumpet-shaped flowers at night.
Sacred datura often bloom in spring, but flowers can appear any time of year with
enough rain. The flower emits a foul odor, and all parts of the plant are toxic. But
sacred datura is central to the religious ceremonies of many native tribes. The plant
contains high doses of hallucinogenic alkaloids that native shamans use to induce
visions. Datura ceremonies frequently focus on rites of passage, and the visions
people experience help determine their future roles within the tribe. Even low doses
can be fatal, however, so unless you're a native shaman don't try it.

Prickly Pear
Cactus

Grand Canyon is home to eight species of prickly
pear cactus, which are easily identified by flat,
green pads covered in prickly nodules or spines. Vivid
flowers, ranging from bright yellow to magenta, bloom in
spring. Native tribes harvest prickly pear fruit ("tuna") and the
fleshy pads ("nopal"), both of which are popular foods in Mexico
today. Some prickly pear pads are covered in white lumps. These are
cochineal insects, which attach to prickly pear cacti, drink its liquid, and
cover themselves in a sticky white substance for protection. When the bugs
are crushed, they produce a luxurious scarlet color rarely found in nature. Aztec
rulers cherished clothes stained red with cochineal, and following the conquest of
Mexico dried cochineal became the country's second-most valuable export after
silver. The red dye colored everything from British military uniforms to American
flags. Cochineal is still used today as a natural red dye in foods and cosmetics under
the names "carmine" or "natural red 4."

Pinyon-Juniper Woodlands

Pinyon pines and junipers are two of the most common trees in the West, covering roughly 100 million acres from Oregon to northern Mexico. Pinyon-juniper woodlands, which are found on both rims of Grand Canyon, cover eight percent of Grand Canyon National Park.

Utah Juniper
Juniperus osteosperma

Juniper trees are easily identified by their stringy bark, scaly green shoots, and tiny blue "berries." Distillers use juniper berries (which are actually tiny modified pine cones) to give gin its herbal flavor. The word "juniper" is actually derived from *genever,* the Dutch word for gin. Berries used in gin-making traditionally come from the common juniper, not the Utah juniper found in Grand Canyon. Growing up to 30 feet tall, Utah junipers send out deep roots in search of water. Tap roots can penetrate 25 feet, while lateral roots spread out 100 feet or more. This impressive root system accounts for up to two-thirds of the tree's total mass, allowing some junipers to grow even if they have been toppled over by wind. Under optimal conditions junipers can live over 1,000 years. Though not as important as pinyon pines to native tribes, juniper trees still had many important uses. Women fashioned the soft, stringy bark into clothing, including baby diapers. And because juniper wood burns evenly with a steady flame, it is considered one of the best woods for cooking fires.

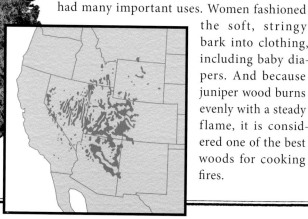

Pinyon Pine

Pinyon pines are one of the most important food sources on the Colorado Plateau. Native tribes, modern foragers, and wild animals all enjoy pinyon pine nuts, which are nutritious, delicious, and can be harvested in enormous quantities. There are two species of pinyon pine in Grand Canyon: Colorado pinyons (*Pinus edulis*), which have two needles, and singleleaf pinyons (*Pinus monophylla*), the only pine tree in the world with just one needle per fascicle. Both evolved from Mexican pines around 20 million years ago. As pinyon pines spread north, their nuts became a favorite food of pinyon jays, which gathered nuts by the thousands and buried them for later use. Leftover or forgotten nuts grew into new trees, and over millions of years pinyons evolved new characteristics based on the kinds of nuts the birds preferred. Most pine trees produce small nuts with "wings" so the wind can disperse the seeds. Pinyon nuts, by contrast, became large and "wingless," and pinyon pines are now completely dependent on pinyon jays and other animals to spread their seeds far from the tree. When humans arrived in the Southwest, they quickly recognized the nutritional importance of pinyon pines. In late summer, when the nuts ripen, native tribes harvested and stored as many nuts as possible. Pinyon pines can grow 50 feet or taller, and pine cones on the highest branches were knocked down with long poles. Pine nuts were removed from the cones and roasted, boiled, or ground into flour on stone metates. During harsh winters, an adequate supply of pinyon nuts could mean the difference between life and death. Sticky pinyon pine pitch was also used to waterproof baskets and storage containers.

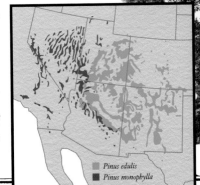

Pinus edulis
Pinus monophylla

Quaking Aspen
Populus tremuloides

Quaking aspen have the widest range of any tree in North America, spanning 47 degrees of latitude (over half the distance from the equator to the North Pole), 110 degrees of longitude (from Alaska to Newfoundland), and elevations ranging from sea level to 12,000 feet. In the Grand Canyon region aspen often grow at altitudes above 7,000 feet. The tree's flat leaves, which attach to branches via long stems called petioles, tremble and quake at the slightest breeze, hence the name *quaking* aspen. In October, when the leaves turn bright yellow, entire hillsides shimmer with gold. Aspen are aggressive colonizers that grow quickly in the wake of forest fires. The forests on Grand Canyon's North Rim, which have burned repeatedly over the past few decades, are filled with young aspen trees. Autumn foliage is spectacular on the North Rim, and it will only get better as these aspen continue to grow. Many aspen are less than 50 feet tall, but they can grow as high as 130 feet. Because their trunks are thin and white, they are sometimes mistaken for birch trees. But birch trees have peeling white bark while aspen trees have smooth white bark with black patches. Aspen bark can photosynthesize, and when wet it turns slightly green. Animals such as deer and elk eat the bark, twigs, and leaves. Aspen reproduce through both seeds and root sprouts, but root sprouts, which are clones of the original tree, are the dominant form of reproduction. Although individual trees often live less than 150 years, root systems can live for thousands of years. The world's largest known aspen clone, located in central Utah, has 47,000 stems, covers over 100 acres, and is estimated to weigh over 13 million pounds. The clone, called Pando, is considered the world's largest living organism.

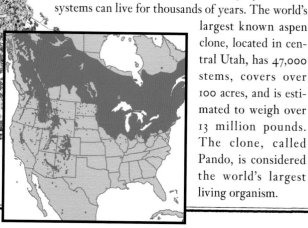

Ponderosa Pine
Pinus ponderosa

Ponderosa pines are the most widely distributed pine species in North America, growing from Canada to Mexico. In the U.S. they are found in every Western state. In Grand Canyon they grow on both rims and cover about two percent of the park. Ponderosa pines are easily identified by their height (they can grow 150 feet or taller), long needles (up to eight inches in bundles of three), and thick, plate-like bark. If you still aren't sure, put your nose in the bark's cracks. If it smells like vanilla or butterscotch, it's a ponderosa pine. The tree is named for its heavy wood (*ponderosa* is Spanish for "heavy"), which is prized as lumber. Ponderosa pines can survive low-intensity fires thanks to thick bark, and mature trees are sometimes charred near the base. Far from a threat, small fires are essential to ponderosa health. Fire clears out competing species that would otherwise encroach on ponderosa habitat. Only enormous fires that burn the crown can kill a mature ponderosa. Older trees often drop lower branches to prevent fire from climbing the tree and reaching the vulnerable crown. Ponderosas can even survive lightning strikes, which flash-boil the sap and blow off chunks of bark, sending energy away from the tree. As ponderosa pines grow older, the bark changes color. Young trees have black bark, while older trees have yellowish bark. Early settlers did not realize the black and yellow trunks belonged to the same species, which is why ponderosas pines are sometimes called blackjack pine or yellow pine. Under ideal conditions ponderosa pines can live 600 years or longer.

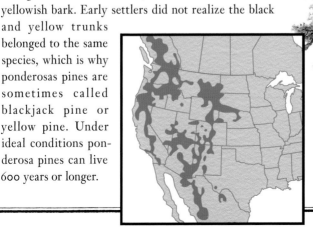

Grand Canyon Birds

Over 440 bird species have been identified in Grand Canyon, roughly ten percent of which live in the canyon year-round. To learn more about Grand Canyon birds, pick up a copy of *Birds of the Grand Canyon Region*, published by the Grand Canyon Conservancy.

Peregrine Falcon
Falco peregrinus

Peregrine falcons are legendary hunters that can spot birds from thousands of feet above, then dive-bomb them at speeds topping 200 mph—the fastest speed of any animal. The collision creates an explosion of feathers, and victims that don't die upon impact have their necks broken by the peregrine's powerful beak. During World War II, Allied troops trained peregrine falcons to kill Nazi carrier pigeons. By the early 1970s, however, peregrine populations collapsed due to the toxic effects of the pesticide DDT. When ingested by birds, DDT fatally weakened eggshells, and mothers accidentally crushed their own brittle eggs. After DDT was banned, peregrine populations recovered, and in 1999 peregrine falcons were removed from the federal endangered species list. Grand Canyon's steep cliffs offer ideal peregrine habitat. Today the park is home to the largest peregrine falcon population in America.

Canyon Wren
Catherpes mexicanus

This small brown and white songbird is famous for its beautiful call, a series of delicate high-pitched whistles that descend in speed and tone. Spend some time in Grand Canyon and you'll likely hear the canyon wren's melodic song. Nests are often built in rocky crevices, and males sing to defend their nesting territory. Canyon wrens are found in the mountains and canyons of the arid West, from British Columbia to southern Mexico. Their long, narrow bills are used to pluck insects and spiders from small openings and crevices. Canyon wrens, which are not known to drink water, are believed to get all of their liquids from insects.

Turkey Vulture
Cathartes aura

Turkey vultures are among the world's most successful scavengers, feeding on carrion (dead animals) detected using keen eyesight and a powerful sense of smell. Wingspans that measure up to six feet allow turkey vultures to soar over large areas in search of food. Their bald, featherless heads enable easy cleaning after poking around a bloody carcass. Turkey vultures (also called buzzards) range from Canada to Argentina. In Grand Canyon they are sometimes mistaken for California condors, but turkey vultures have white feathers on the outer edges of their wings while condors have black feathers on the outer edges of their wings. Both male and female turkey vultures are identical in plumage and similar in size. Adults weigh up to five pounds and can live 16 years in the wild.

Mexican Spotted Owl
Strix occidentalis lucida

These beautiful owls, which range from the southern Rocky Mountains to central Mexico, are one of three spotted owl subspecies in North America. In the 20th century, however, habitat loss led to steep population declines. By 1994 barely 2,000 Mexican spotted owls remained. Today, despite decades of recovery efforts, Mexican spotted owls remain listed as a threatened species. In Grand Canyon they nest in caves and narrow side canyons. During the day they roost in trees or on rock ledges, and at night they hunt small mammals such as woodrats and pocket gophers. Large eyes provide superior vision in low light. Unlike most owls, which have yellow or orange eyes, Mexican spotted owls have dark eyes. Growing up to 19 inches long with a nearly four-foot wingspan, Mexican spotted owls are among the largest owls in North America. Adults can live about 15 years in the wild, and mating pairs are monogamous. Owlets less than five months old sport a soft, downy coat.

Mexican Spotted Owlet

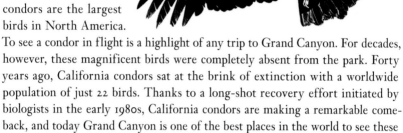

California Condor
Gymnogyps californianus

With wingspans over nine feet, California condors are the largest birds in North America. To see a condor in flight is a highlight of any trip to Grand Canyon. For decades, however, these magnificent birds were completely absent from the park. Forty years ago, California condors sat at the brink of extinction with a worldwide population of just 22 birds. Thanks to a long-shot recovery effort initiated by biologists in the early 1980s, California condors are making a remarkable comeback, and today Grand Canyon is one of the best places in the world to see these enormous birds.

Although cursed with a face that only a mother could love, condors are extremely graceful in flight. Riding thermals, they can fly for hours without ever flapping their wings. Condors can soar as high as 15,000 feet, reach top speeds of 50 mph, and travel hundreds of miles per day. In Grand Canyon, condors are often seen soon after sunrise or just before sunset. Although easily confused with turkey vultures, condors have larger wingspans and triangular white coloring on the underside of their wings. Condors soar gracefully on flat outstreched wings, while turkey vultures often fly with their wings in a wobbly V-shape. Adult condors are characterized by a pink-orange head and a white underwing coloration. Young condors are almost entirely black. Mature condors weigh up to 23 pounds and can live 50 years or more.

California condors are scavengers that feed exclusively on dead animals. Powerful bills break bones and tear out flesh, and bald heads allow the birds to dig deep into bloody carcasses without dirtying their feathers. Condors typically feed on elk, mule deer, and cattle, but they eat just about anything they can find. Because carrion supply is unpredictable, condors eat as much as possible whenever they can. They store excess meat in their "crop," a fleshy extension of the esophagus, visible on the chest, that can hold more than three pounds of meat. Condors can go two weeks without eating if no food is available.

California condors once ranged across North America. During the Ice Age, they feasted on the carcasses of large animals such as mastodons and giant sloths. When those animals went extinct

California
condor range

roughly 10,000 years ago, California condors lost a major food source, and their population began to decline. By the time European explorers arrived, condors lived only in western North America. When western North America was settled, condor populations plummeted due to hunting, egg collecting, the ingestion of poisonous bait (left for coyotes), and the ingestion of poisonous lead shot from the carcasses of hunted animals. Condors generally lay just one egg every two years, and this slow reproductive rate exacerbated the population decline. By the 1940s, condors were only found in southern California.

In 1982 the worldwide California condor population dropped to just 22 birds. In desperation, the Los Angeles Zoo and the San Diego Zoo started a controversial captive breeding program. In 1987 biologists captured the last wild condors to ensure their safety. One year later, the first captive-bred California condor hatched. The chick was fed using a condor mother hand puppet, which prevented it from growing accustomed to humans—a critical factor if the young condor was to someday survive in the wild.

In 1992 biologists reintroduced the first captive-raised condors to central California. Four years later, biologists reintroduced condors to the Vermillion Cliffs in northern Arizona, and shortly thereafter condors were flying over Grand Canyon for the first time in over seven decades. Grand Canyon's remote location, rugged terrain, and strong updrafts offer ideal conditions for condors, and over the next two decades more captive-bred condors were released in the region. In 2003 a wild-bred condor chick successfully fledged in Grand Canyon—the first time a wild condor had fledged anywhere in the world since 1982. Since then multiple wild condors have fledged in Arizona and Utah.

Today there are roughly 500 California condors, over half of which live in the wild. Although lead poisoning from spent bullets remains the biggest threat to wild California condors, groups like the Peregrine Fund (peregrinefund.org) are working hard to ensure a bright future for these magnificent birds.

Bighorn Sheep
Ovis canadensis

Bighorn sheep are among Grand Canyon's most impressive animals. Well adapted to steep terrain, they can traverse two-inch ledges, scramble up steep slopes, and jump down 20-foot inclines with grace. Their unique concave hooves, which feature a hard outer edge and soft interior sole, help them grip rocks and navigate cliffs. Sharp eyesight and keen hearing help them detect predators such as mountain lions, coyotes, and bobcats.

The ram's legendary horns take up to a decade to grow, curving up and over the ears in a C-shaped curl. A large pair of horns can weigh up to 30 pounds and reach 30 inches in length. During mating season, competing rams charge each other head-on at speeds topping 20 mph. When rams collide, their horns smash together, producing a loud cracking sound that can be heard for miles. Thickened skulls allow rams to withstand repeated collisions. Rams can fight for over 24 hours, and those with the biggest horns generally do the most mating.

Bighorn rams weigh up to 220 pounds. Ewes weigh up to 160 pounds. Both rams and ewes develop horns shortly after birth, but ewe horns are skinny and never grow past half curl. Ewes generally stay with their family herd. Adult rams, by contrast, live largely isolated lives.

Desert bighorn sheep (*Ovis canadensis nelsoni*), which are found in the deserts of the U.S. and Mexico, are a subspecies of bighorn sheep found in much of the West. Well adapted to arid environments, desert bighorns can survive for weeks without water. Grasses constitute the majority of their diet, but they also eat sedges and cacti. Adults can live up to 20 years in the wild. From 1850 to 1950, desert bighorn populations plummeted due to hunting and diseases spread by domestic sheep. Since 1960, however, desert bighorn numbers have increased substantially thanks to successful conservation measures.

Historic Bighorn Range

Historic Desert Bighorn Range

Mountain Lion
Felis concolor

Mountain lions (also known as pumas or cougars) are found from Canada to Argentina—the most extensive range of any land species in the Western Hemisphere. Historically they inhabited much of North America. In the late 1800s and early 1900s, however, mountain lions were hunted to the brink of extinction. Following the enactment of strict hunting regulations, they have made a steady comeback in the West, and today they are slowly spreading east.

Mountain lions are the second-largest wildcats in the Western Hemisphere after jaguars. Males weigh up to 250 pounds and measure more than eight feet in length. Females weigh up to 140 pounds and can measure up to seven feet in length. Mountain lions have proportionally the largest hind legs of any feline. They can jump nearly 20 feet vertically and 40 feet horizontally, and they can run up to 50 mph.. Retractable claws aid in both hunting and tree climbing.

Mountain lions travel up to 25 miles a day in search of food. A mountain lion in Grand Canyon descended the South Rim, swam across the Colorado River, and climbed to the North Rim in just eight hours. Mountain lions are quick, efficient hunters, quietly stalking prey before pouncing. Victims often die from a lethal bite to the spinal cord. In Grand Canyon, mountain lions feed primarily on mule deer, killing up to one per week. Other prey include elk, coyote, and bighorn sheep.

Solitary and territorial, mountain lions require an extensive "home range." In Grand Canyon that range can measure up to 185 square miles. Adult mountain lions meet only to mate. Females are exclusively responsible for parenting, and cubs stay with their mother for roughly two years while she teaches them survival skills. Mountain lions are born with a spotted coloration, which develops into a uniform tan coloration as they mature.

Reclusive by nature, mountain lions go to great lengths to avoid people. Sightings are uncommon, and attacks on humans are extremely rare. If you do encounter a mountain lion in Grand Canyon, slowly back away while holding a steady gaze.

Mountain Lion Range

Elk
Cervus canadensis

Elk are the largest member of the deer family on the Colorado Plateau. Male elk (bulls) grow up to eight feet long and weigh up to 800 pounds. Female elk (cows) grow up to seven feet long and weigh up to 500 pounds. Elk are the second-largest member of the deer family in North America after moose. The name "elk" was derived from a European word for moose because early explorers thought the two animals looked similar.

Elk are distinguished from mule deer by their massive size and unique coloration: a tan body with a dark brown "pelage" (coat) above the neck. Shawnee Indians call elk *wapiti*, "White Rump," due to their white backsides.

In autumn, massive antlers are an elk's most prominent characteristic. Antlers, which grow only on bulls, can reach four feet in length and weigh up to 50 pounds. They are shed each spring, and over the next three to four months new antlers grow back at the rate of about one half-inch per day. Antlers reach maximum size in time for the rut (mating season). During the rut, which generally lasts from late summer to mid-November, bulls emit a bugle-like sound as a sign of dominance and a challenge to other bulls. The bugle starts off as a bellow and changes to a shrill scream. It can often be heard for miles. Dominance between bulls is determined in contests where bulls engage in antler wrestling. The most dominant bulls assemble a harem of a dozen or more cows, which then give birth in the spring. Those that survive to adulthood can live 10 years or more in the wild.

Elk are ruminants with four-chambered stomachs. They forage on grasses, plants, leaves, and bark. On average, elk eat about 20 pounds of vegetation a day. Elk are often seen grazing near Grand Canyon Village. Although they have become accustomed to humans and appear docile, elk should never be approached.

In the early 1900s, elk were eliminated from the Southwest due to over-hunting. The elk found in Grand Canyon today are descendents of elk transplanted from Yellowstone National Park between 1913 and 1928.

Mule Deer
Odocoileus hemionus

Mule deer are named for their large ears, which move independently of each other like those of a mule. Common throughout the western U.S., their range extends from western Canada to central Mexico. They are found in all of Grand Canyon's habitats, from the rim to the river. Adult mule deer are five to seven feet in length. Bucks weigh 150 to 300 pounds, and does weigh 95 to 200 pounds.

Mule deer are ruminants with multi-chambered stomachs. In summer they forage on plants, leaves, and brushy vegetation. In winter they forage on conifers such as juniper and ponderosa pine.

Although closely related to white-tailed deer, mule deer are slightly larger. Mule deer have white tails with a black tip, and their antlers fork as they grow. (White-tailed deer antlers, by contrast, branch from a single main beam.) Bucks grow a large pair of antlers each year, then shed them each winter. This annual cycle of antler growth and shedding is regulated by changes in the length of the day.

During the fall rut, bucks compete for does. Although conflict between bucks is infrequent, mild fights sometimes break out. Fighting bucks often enmesh their antlers and try to force the head of the other buck down. Although injuries are rare, antlers sometimes become locked together. If two bucks cannot unlock their antlers, they will be unable to eat, and both will ultimately die of starvation.

After breeding in fall, gestation lasts 190 to 200 days. Young does give birth to one fawn. Older does often give birth to twins. Fawns are born with white spots on their backs, which help camouflage them with the dappled light of the forest floor. As fawns grow older, the white spots disappear. Fawns are able to distinguish their mother through a unique odor produced by glands on the mother's hind legs. Fawns stay with their mother until they are weaned the following fall. Conflict between does is common, so family groups tend to be spaced widely apart.

Adult mule deer live up to 11 years in the wild. Predators in Grand Canyon include mountain lions, bobcats, and coyotes.

Mule Deer Range

Bobcat
Lynx rufus

Bobcats are North America's most common wildcat. Their range extends from Florida to the desert Southwest, but they are highly elusive animals. They typically spend the day resting, then search for prey around dusk or dawn. Their diet includes a wide range of small animals such as rabbits, squirrels, birds, and snakes. Bobcats rarely chase their prey, however, preferring to seek out a hiding spot and lie in wait. When a victim approaches, the bobcat pounces, snagging its prey with sharp, retractable claws. The name "bobcat" comes from the cat's stubby "bobbed" tail. Bobcats share many personality traits with house cats, including hissing, purring, and using trees as scratching posts. Like most felines, bobcats are largely solitary. Males and females meet only to mate. Females generally have litters of two or three kittens, and those that reach adulthood live six to eight years in the wild. Adult bobcats weigh an average of 20 pounds.

Coyote
Canis latrans

Historically found in the open spaces of the West, coyotes greatly expanded their range following the extermination of wolves in the 1800s. Today coyotes are found throughout most of North America. Intelligent and adaptable, they live in every ecological zone in Grand Canyon, from deserts at the bottom of the canyon to spruce-fir forests on the North Rim. Coyotes typically hunt in pairs, and when chasing prey they can reach speeds topping 40 mph. Their diet consists mostly of small mammals, but coyotes eat just about anything, including birds, snakes, insects, and trash. Adult coyotes weigh up to 30 pounds. In winter, their brownish-red coat turns grey. In native legends Coyote is often portrayed as a scheming, meddling trickster who scrapes by on cunning and charm. The word "coyote" is derived from the Nahuatl (Aztec) word *cóyotl*. Coyote's Latin name, *Canis latrans*, means "barking dog."

Squirrels & Chipmunks

Say hello to the most dangerous animals in Grand Canyon. Some visitors worry about mountain lions, scorpions, or rattlesnakes, but squirrels and chipmunks are actually the number one cause of human-animal injuries in the park. Unlike mountain lions, scorpions, and rattlesnakes, which are smart enough to avoid people, some people are not smart enough to avoid squirrels and chipmunks. Instead, they try to feed the adorable critters, who respond by biting the person's hand, resulting in blood, stitches—even disease.

Rock Squirrel

Squirrels and chipmunks also chew through unattended backpacks and tents if they smell food inside. In Grand Canyon there are five chipmunk species and five squirrel species, most notably the Kaibab squirrel (below). Chipmunks are smaller than squirrels, rarely growing longer than ten inches. Both squirrels and chipmunks can have stripes running down their sides, but only chipmunks have stripes on their faces.

Uinta Chipmunk

Kaibab Squirrel
Sciurus aberti kaibabensis

These beautiful squirrels are found only in the ponderosa pine forests of the Kaibab Plateau, an area that measures roughly 20 miles by 40 miles on Grand Canyon's North Rim. In behavior and biology, Kaibab squirrels are nearly identical to Abert's squirrels, which are common on the South Rim. But whereas Abert's squirrels have a white belly and gray tail, Kaibab squirrels have a dark belly and white tail. Scientists believe both squirrels once belonged to the same species. When global temperatures fluctuated during the Ice Age, however, ecological zones shifted and an isolated Abert's squirrel population was confined to the Kaibab Plateau. Over time those isolated squirrels evolved into a distinct subspecies. Both Kaibab squirrels and Abert's squirrels depend on ponderosa pines as a source of food, eating the tender bark as well as seeds from pine cones.

Grand Canyon Pink Rattlesnake
Crotalus viridis abyssus

Grand Canyon is home to six rattlesnake species, including the Grand Canyon Pink rattlesnake, which has a pale, pinkish coloration and irregular dark blotches with a pale center. A subspecies of Western rattlesnakes, the Grand Canyon Pink rattlesnake is found only in Grand Canyon. Rattlesnakes have poor eyesight but a sharp sense of smell. They detect body heat through infrared sensors on either side of their heads. These keen senses are used to detect prey while the snake lies in wait. When a rattlesnake strikes, it injects a paralyzing venom through sharp fangs, then swallows the motionless victim whole. Rattlesnakes, in turn, are preyed upon by eagles and hawks, which pluck snakes from the ground and drop them repeatedly from the air. Other rattlesnake species in Grand Canyon include the Great Basin rattlesnake, Hopi rattlesnake, Mojave rattlesnake, Speckled rattlesnake, and Black-Tailed rattlesnake.

Gila Monster
Heloderma suspectum

The largest lizards in North America, Gila monsters grow up to two feet long and weigh up to four pounds. Their range extends from southwest Utah to northwest Mexico, including the deserts in western Grand Canyon. Gila (pronounced *HEE-la*) monsters are the only venomous lizards native to the U.S., but they are slow, sluggish animals that pose little threat to humans. The name "Gila" refers to the Gila River in Arizona, where the lizards were first documented. The "monster" epithet likely comes from the exaggerated beliefs of early settlers, who claimed the lizard had a poisonous breath, vice-like jaws, and a fatal bite. Although no deaths have ever been confirmed from Gila monsters, their venom is among the most painful of any reptile. It has been described as "hot lava coursing through your veins." Gila monsters prey on small birds, mammals and insects, and they are fond of bird and reptile eggs. Gila monster predators include coyotes and hawks. The lizard's scientific name, *Heloderma*, means "studded skin." Its bright pink or yellow coloration likely serves as a defensive warning.

Tarantulas

Tarantulas are the world's largest spiders, and they are common throughout the desert Southwest. Grand Canyon is home to the Grand Canyon black tarantula, which measures up to four inches long. Tarantulas eat anything they can chase down, including insects, lizards, and small mammals. They inject prey with paralyzing venom, then secrete a digestive enzyme to liquefy the victim's internal organs. The tarantula then sucks out the organ soup with its straw-like mouth. Although painful, tarantula bites are harmless to humans. Tarantulas are most active during fall mating season, when male tarantulas wander in search of female burrows.

Tarantula Hawk
Pepsis thisbe

This large wasp, which grows up to two inches long, is a tarantula's worst nightmare. After stinging a tarantula with paralyzing venom, a female tarantula hawk drags the spider back to its burrow, lays her eggs on its body, and seals the burrow—burying the spider alive. When wasp larvae hatch, they feast on the still-living tarantula, munching on non-essential body parts first to maximize freshness by keeping the spider alive as long as possible.

Arizona Bark Scorpion
Centruroides sculpturatus

Grand Canyon is home to the most venomous scorpion in North America—the Arizona bark scorpion, whose sting causes severe pain for up to 72 hours. Fortunately, scorpions are nocturnal and rarely encountered, and their sting is rarely fatal. Only two people have died from scorpion stings in Arizona since 1968. Bark scorpions grow up to three inches long. Unlike many scorpions, bark scorpions can climb trees, hence their name. They have six eyes on the side of their head and two eyes on top. Their famous stinger, located at the tip of the tail, is thrust over the head to stab victims and inject venom. Scorpion prey includes insects and lizards. Scorpions are preyed upon, in turn, by owls, bats, and tarantulas. A scorpion mother gives birth to live young, who ride on her back until their first molt.

HISTORY

HUMANS FIRST SET eyes on Grand Canyon around 12,000 years ago, when early hunter-gatherers arrived in the Southwest. Little is known about these prehistoric people, but small artifacts found in caves confirm their existence in Grand Canyon. Among the objects discovered were spear points and small split-twig figurines twisted into animal shapes. The figurines were often made from a single willow twig, split down the middle and twisted to resemble deer or bighorn sheep, then pierced with a tiny agave spear. Archaeologists believe these figurines were totems used in hunting rituals.

What ultimately happened to these early people is unclear. It's possible they abandoned Grand Canyon, but it's just as likely they stayed. In either case, a new culture called the Ancestral Puebloans (aka Anasazi) appeared several thousand years later. Ancestral Puebloans occupied the Four Corners region from roughly 1500 B.C. to A.D. 1250. For over two thousand years they flourished in and around Grand Canyon, which marked the westernmost range of their territory.

Archaeologists subdivide Ancestral Puebloans into two cultural periods: Basketmaker, from 1500 B.C. to A.D. 750, and Pueblo, from A.D. 750 to 1250. Basketmakers wove plant fibers into beautiful baskets, clothing, and sandals. Although they started out as hunter-gatherers, Basketmakers eventually adopted agriculture, which spread north from Mexico. They constructed dwellings in caves or under overhanging cliffs, growing beans, corn, and squash nearby.

Farming became the Basketmakers' main source of food, but they continued hunting animals with atlatls (leveraged throwing spears). Animals provided both food and raw materials for clothing. In winter, Basketmakers wore robes made of deer skin, rabbit skin, or turkey feathers. In summer they wore loincloths and skirts woven from plant fibers. Extensive trade routes provided additional goods, including seashells from the Pacific Coast and live parrots from Mexico. The Basketmakers kept dogs as pets, smoked tobacco from pipes, and played music on flutes. By A.D. 600 they also adopted pottery, which allowed them to boil liquids and cook soups in ceramic vessels over open fires.

Split-twig figurine

Around A.D. 700 Basketmakers adopted the bow and arrow, which allowed them to hunt more food in less time. Pottery also flourished, which meant less time weaving baskets. More free time led to cultural and technological advances, which ushered in the Pueblo period. Ancestral Puebloans built dwellings with stone masonry, constructed irrigation ditches near fertile areas, and stored surplus crops in granaries (stone storage compartments).

As Ancestral Puebloan life grew in complexity, so did the rules governing their society. Customs and social codes became highly structured, and a few large settlements began operating like independent city-states. Artistic achievements also blossomed. Ancestral Puebloans wove beautiful cotton clothes, covered dwellings with murals and pictographs, and designed elaborate costumes for religious ceremonies.

By A.D. 1100 Ancestral Puebloans occupied thousands of sites in and around Grand Canyon. Farther west, they built impressive cliff dwellings and six-story structures—the tallest buildings in America until skyscrapers appeared in the 1880s. The technological achievements of the Ancestral Puebloans placed them among the most advanced civilizations north of Mexico.

Then, near the height of their prosperity, Ancestral Puebloans abandoned their settlements and vanished from Grand Canyon. Archaeologists are at a loss to explain the mystery of this swift departure. Some believe Ancestral Puebloans fell victim to a massive drought. Others blame a depletion of natural resources. Still others think there was a great war between neighboring tribes.

Unfortunately, little evidence remains to provide a clear picture of what actually happened. We do know that many Ancestral Puebloans moved south and merged with the Hopi and Zuni tribes. Within a few centuries, other tribes including the Havasupai, Hualapai, Southern Paiute, and Navajo had also settled the Grand Canyon region.

Ancestral Puebloan
Pottery

Mystery of the
Ancestral Puebloans

THE SWIFT DECLINE of the Ancestral Puebloans is the Southwest's greatest archaeological mystery. Why would a culture at the height of its prosperity—by many accounts the most advanced civilization north of Mexico—suddenly abandon its settlements? What caused them to leave the Four Corners region they had occupied for over 2,000 years, never to return?

Some archaeologists believe the Ancestral Puebloans fell victim to a massive drought. The Southwest experienced an extended period of decreased rainfall in the late 1200s, and it seems logical to connect this with Ancestral Puebloan decline. But recent evidence suggests the so-called Great Drought may not have been great enough to cause complete cultural collapse. Ancestral Puebloans, it turns out, started to abandon their settlements prior to the drought. And they had survived worse droughts in the past. Why should this one be different?

Some archaeologists believe the abandonment was triggered by a depletion of the region's scarce natural resources, which could have led to social and political upheaval—possibly even war. Some Ancestral Puebloan structures built near the end appear to be defensive in nature. But if there was a war, why didn't the winners stay to enjoy the spoils?

Finally, some archaeologists think the Ancestral Puebloans' demise was triggered by religious collapse. Religion and daily life were one and the same to Ancestral Puebloans, and a collapse of one could have triggered a collapse of the other. Faced with failing crops and chronic shortages, Ancestral Puebloans may have simply lost faith. At the same time, the Hopi's new Katsina religion was gaining momentum nearby. With its colorful masks and lurid dances, the Katsina religion may have lured Ancestral Puebloans away.

While each of these theories offers a possible explanation, many unanswered questions remain. Until new evidence comes to light, the mystery of the Ancestral Puebloans will remain one of Grand Canyon's best-kept secrets.

Left: Ancestral Puebloan baby diaper fashioned out of juniper bark. Right: Ancestral Puebloan sandal made out of woven yucca fiber.

HOPI

The Hopi are one of Grand Canyon's oldest tribes, having lived in northeast Arizona for over 1,000 years. Oraibi, a Hopi village east of Grand Canyon, was first settled around A.D. 1050, making it the oldest continuously inhabited town in the United States. The Hopi are descendants of Ancestral Puebloans, whom they call *Hisatsinom* ("Ancient Ones").

Grand Canyon is sacred to the Hopi, who believe both people and animals emerged into the present universe from the *Sipapuni*, a mineral spring near the junction of *Pisis'vayu* (the Colorado River) and *Palavayu* (the Little Colorado River) at the bottom of the canyon. Some Hopi men make multi-day pilgrimages to the Sipapuni, offering foods and prayers to provide safe passage. Hopi women, guardians of future generations, are culturally discouraged from entering the depths of Grand Canyon.

Kachinas (*Ka*, "respect," *china* "spirit") play an important role in Hopi religion. These benign spirit beings, who reside in the San Francisco Peaks north of Flagstaff, visit Hopi villages between the *Soyál* winter solstice and the *Niman Kachina* summer solstice. Hopi craftsmen carve brightly painted wooden dolls to represent different Kachinas. These dolls help Hopi children learn about hundreds of Kachinas, which represent different aspects of the natural world.

Hopi ceremonies often coincide with agricultural cycles. The most famous is the *Chu'tiva* (Snake-Antelope Dance), where dancers put live snakes in their mouths to summon rain for a bountiful harvest. During summer solstice, Hopi girls embark on a four-day puberty ceremony where their hair is decorated in an intricate "squash blossom" style. Hopi maidens can wear squash blossoms until marriage, at which point they often wear long braids down the back.

Today roughly 10,000 Hopi live among three mesas and 13 villages on their 1.5-million-acre reservation, located east of Grand Canyon.

NAVAJO

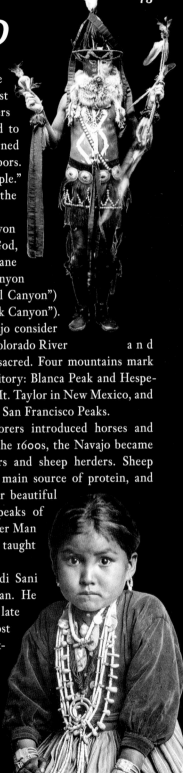

The Navajo were one of the last tribes to settle the Grand Canyon region, arriving from northwest Canada around 600 years ago. Hunter-gatherers unaccustomed to the desert, the Navajo resorted to raiding other tribes. Eventually, however, they learned to grow corn, beans, and squash from their neighbors. They refer to themselves as *Dine'é*, "The People." Navajo, a name given by the Spanish, is based on the Puebloan word *navahū* ("fields next to a ravine").

According to Navajo legend, Grand Canyon formed when *Ghąą' Ask'idii*, the Humpback God, stood in the center of earth and dragged his cane across the ground. Navajo names for Grand Canyon include *Tsé'Chíí' Koo'* ("Red Wall Canyon") and *Tsékooh Hatsaa'* ("Big Rock Canyon").

Like the Hopi, the Navajo consider the confluence of the Colorado River and Little Colorado River sacred. Four mountains mark traditional Navajo territory: Blanca Peak and Hesperus Peak in Colorado, Mt. Taylor in New Mexico, and *Dook'o'oosłííd*, Arizona's San Francisco Peaks.

After Spanish explorers introduced horses and sheep to the region in the 1600s, the Navajo became expert horseback riders and sheep herders. Sheep replaced deer as their main source of protein, and wool replaced cotton for beautiful woven rugs. Legend speaks of two animal beings, Spider Man and Spider Woman, who taught the Navajo how to build looms and weave.

In the mid-1800s a Navajo man named Atsidi Sani learned silversmithing from a Mexican craftsman. He taught the skill to other Navajo, and by the late 1800s they added turquoise to their work. The most famous Navajo design is the squash blossom necklace (pictured above).

Today there are over 300,000 Navajo, nearly two-thirds of whom live on the 27,000-square-mile Navajo Reservation, which spans parts of Arizona, New Mexico, and Utah.

HAVASUPAI & HUALAPAI

The Havasupai have lived in Grand Canyon for over 700 years. Their territory once covered much of the South Rim, extending from Havasu Canyon east to the Little Colorado River. The name *Havasupai*, "People of the Blue-Green Water," refers to the beautiful turquoise pools and waterfalls in Havasu Canyon (p.283), Grand Canyon's largest side canyon. Over 500 Havasupai currently live in the village of Supai, located 2,000 feet below the rim of Havasu Canyon. Because they have access to constant water, the Havasupai historically grew more food than any other tribe in the region. Havasu Creek, one of the most dependable water sources in Grand Canyon, helped the Havasupai weather even the greatest droughts. Indian Garden, located 3,000 feet below present-day Grand Canyon Village, was another important water source where the Havasupai grew crops during the sunny summer months. In winter, when the narrow walls of Havasu Canyon let in just a few hours of sunlight each day, the tribe migrated to the rim to gather plants and hunt animals.

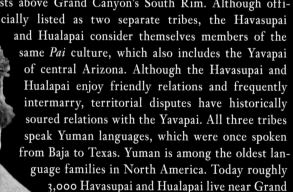

The *Hualapai*, "Ponderosa Pine People," historically occupied the vast pine forests above Grand Canyon's South Rim. Although officially listed as two separate tribes, the Havasupai and Hualapai consider themselves members of the same *Pai* culture, which also includes the Yavapai of central Arizona. Although the Havasupai and Hualapai enjoy friendly relations and frequently intermarry, territorial disputes have historically soured relations with the Yavapai. All three tribes speak Yuman languages, which were once spoken from Baja to Texas. Yuman is among the oldest language families in North America. Today roughly 3,000 Havasupai and Hualapai live near Grand Canyon, many in the town of Peach Springs, Arizona.

SOUTHERN PAIUTE

The Southern Paiute settled the region north of Grand Canyon around A.D. 1300. Their historic range, which once covered 40,000 square miles from eastern California to the Four Corners, consists of harsh desert surrounded by forested peaks and plateaus. By moving seasonally through a variety of elevations, they enjoyed a wide variety of edible plants and wild game. They refer to themselves as *Nüwü* ("Indigenous People"). "Paiute" comes from the words *paa ets* ("Water People"), a reference to their tendency to gather near springs and streams. Where water was plentiful, they cultivated corn, beans, and squash.

The Kaibab Band of Southern Paiute occupied the forested plateau above Grand Canyon's North Rim. *Taváts* the Wolf is said to have given them their homeland, which they call *Neung'we Tuvip*. Kaibab is derived from the Paiute word *Kaivavits*, which means "Mountain Lying Down." The Southern Paiute call Grand Canyon *Piyapaxa 'Uipi*, and they descended trails into the canyon to trade with South Rim tribes. Although the Southern Paiute enjoyed good relations with the Havasupai and Hualapai, they suffered brutal raids from the Navajo, who often captured women and children as slaves.

A highly mobile people, the Southern Paiute preferred flexible woven baskets to fragile pottery. Basketry was a female skill passed down from mother to daughter. Tightly woven cooking baskets, into which women dropped hot rocks to boil liquids, required the greatest skill to make.

When famed explorer John Wesley Powell (p.87) first visited Grand Canyon, he enlisted the help of Kaibab Paiute leader Chuarrumpeak (whose name means "Brains") to help him navigate the rugged landscape. Today roughly 2,500 members of the Southern Paiute tribe live in Arizona, Nevada, and Utah.

THE SPANISH QUEST FOR GOLD

WHEN SPANISH CONQUISTADOR Hernán Cortés defeated the Aztecs in 1519, it set in motion the colonization of North America. Spain's sprawling empire soon covered much of the New World, but maintaining those far-flung properties required enormous resources. Despite vast wealth plundered from the Aztecs, Spain was soon desperate for additional funds.

In 1529 a Spanish vessel shipwrecked off the Florida coast. Its four survivors spent the next seven years wandering across North America, and when they finally reached New Spain (Mexico) they told stories of fabulous cities of gold located somewhere in the American Southwest. The cities, referred to as the Seven Cities of Cibola, quickly captured the Spanish imagination.

In 1540 Spanish authorities organized a military expedition to locate the Seven Cities of Cibola. Led by 29-year-old Francisco Vázquez de Coronado, the expedition consisted of 300 Spanish men, several hundred natives, and thousands of cattle, sheep, and goats. Five months later the expedition reached the spot where the Seven Cities were rumored to be located. All they found was a small village.

Coronado was dejected, but the villagers told him of a larger group of seven cities to the west. Coronado dispatched his lieutenant, Don Pedro de Tovar, to investigate their claims. When Tovar returned, he reported that he had failed to locate the Seven Cites of Cibola, but he had learned of a mighty river to the west. Hoping the river was the gateway to Cibola, Coronado dispatched another search party under the command of García López de Cárdenas.

After three weeks of harrowing travel, Cárdenas' party became the first white men to view Grand Canyon. They were hardly impressed. From their vantage point on the South Rim—believed to be somewhere between present-day Moran Point and Desert View—the Spaniards estimated the Colorado River to be just six feet wide. Their Hopi guides insisted the river was much larger (the average width of the Colorado in Grand Canyon is closer to 300 feet), but the Spaniards refused to believe them. They had never encountered a natural landmark so vast, and they were unable to comprehend its true dimensions.

For three days the Spaniards tried to find a route to the river. One group of soldiers made it one-third of the way down the canyon, but they were unable to descend farther. The soldiers were shocked to discover that rocks that appeared only a few feet high from the rim were actually taller than the 185-foot tower of Seville in Spain. Suddenly comprehending Grand Canyon's true dimensions, Cárdenas turned his men around. Coronado's expedition traveled as far as present-day Kansas, but the Seven Cities of Cibola were never found.

In the decades following Coronado's expedition, Spain once again ignored the American Southwest. No colonization attempts were made until 1598, when Juan de Onate founded Santa Fe, New Mexico. Within a few decades, Spanish missions spread west towards Hopi towns.

The Hopi resented the proselytizing missionaries, who sometimes engaged in violent oppression. In 1680 leaders from several local tribes met in secret to plan a coordinated attack against the Spanish. The Pueblo Revolt, as it was later called, drove out the Spaniards and allowed native tribes to regain control of their territories. But the victory was short-lived. Twelve years later, a more powerful Spanish army marched north to reconquer the territory. As the army approached, the Hopi retreated to tall mesas that were easily defended from above.

While battles raged east of Grand Canyon, tribes in remote western Grand Canyon remained relatively undisturbed. Then, in 1776, a Franciscan missionary named Francisco Tomás Garcés attempted to blaze a trail between the Spanish missions in California and the missions along the Rio Grande. His journey led him up the Colorado River into western Grand Canyon, where he encountered the Havasupai tribe. The Havasupai invited Garcés to stay for five days of feasting—an offer he gladly accepted. When the feast was over, Garcés traveled east towards Hopi territory. But the Hopi, stung by years of warfare with the Spanish, were deeply suspicious of Garcés. They refused to accept his gifts or even sell him corn. Taking the hint, Garcés returned to Havasu Canyon, where he was greeted with yet another multi-day feast.

Not long after Garcés' journey, another Spanish expedition, the Dominguez-Escalante party, left New Mexico to find a northern route to the Pacific Ocean. By the time they reached the Sierra Nevada Mountains, however, deep snows made the mountains impassable. Forced to abandon their mission, the Spaniards headed south, at one point crossing the Colorado River near the northern tip of Grand Canyon. The Dominguez-Escalante party became the third and final Spanish expedition to visit Grand Canyon.

Although the Spanish had relatively little contact with tribes living near Grand Canyon, their indirect presence had a huge impact on native life. The Spanish introduced horses, cattle, and sheep to North America—animals that quickly became vital to the cultures of many Southwestern tribes. The Spanish also introduced new fruits such as peaches, melons, and figs. But along with these positive influences came deadly European diseases like smallpox, which had a devastating impact on native populations.

AMERICAN EXPLORERS

IN 1821 MEXICO won independence from Spain and acquired much of the American Southwest. But Mexico, like Spain, generally avoided the desolate region, and Grand Canyon's native tribes remained relatively undisturbed. Yet a new power was looming on the eastern horizon.

Following the 1803 Louisiana Purchase, American beaver trappers fanned out across the West. Before long they were scouring the wild streams that tumbled down from the Rocky Mountains into the desert Southwest. Grand Canyon, however, was generally avoided as a destination. Although beavers lived at the bottom of the canyon, reaching them proved too arduous a task.

Not that some mountain men didn't try. In 1826 a trapping party led by Ewing Young traveled up the Colorado River on foot, becoming the first Americans to visit Grand Canyon. But their journey was a miserable one. At one point the men plodded through 18 inches of snow and ate tree bark to fend off starvation. Not surprisingly, they found little to like about the region. As one trapper put it: "We arrived where the river emerges from these horrid mountains, which so cage it up, as to deprive all human beings of the ability to descend to its banks, and make use of its waters."

Such descriptions did little to encourage further exploration. With its extreme climate, physically challenging terrain, and striking lack of water, the Four Corners region was a terrible place to settle—which was exactly what attracted the Mormons.

Fleeing religious persecution in Illinois, Brigham Young led his followers to Utah's Great Salt Lake in 1846. The desolate landscape, which was still outside the boundaries of the United States, offered the perfect refuge for the Mormons—a place where they could practice their religion in peace. Over the next two decades, Mormon settlements spread south, representing the first significant white presence anywhere near Grand Canyon. But even the notoriously rugged Mormons refused to explore the depths of Grand Canyon. That job would fall to a one-armed, 34-year-old geology professor named John Wesley Powell.

THE ILL-FATED EXPLORER

In 1857 THE U.S. War Department sent novice Lieutenant Joseph Ives on an expedition to explore the lower reaches of the Colorado River. Unfortunately for Ives, the expedition's 50-foot steamboat, *The Explorer*, was poorly designed to handle the rapids, shallows, and sandbars of the Colorado River. The boat ran aground countless times, and the crew was often forced to unload and tow the boat by hand. After two months of slow progress and much towing, *The Explorer* struck a boulder near the present site of Hoover Dam. The crew was tossed overboard and the boat was wrecked beyond repair.

Defeated, Ives declared that he had reached the farthest navigable point on the Colorado River. Not only was his statement untrue, but Ives had already been proven wrong. Several weeks earlier, a man named George Johnson, incensed at being passed over by the War Department to lead the historic journey, had steamed his own boat past the point where *The Explorer* wrecked.

Ives' expedition produced several fine maps of the region, but much of the Colorado River remained a mystery. Writing in his log, Ives concluded his journey with the unfortunate remark: "The region is, of course, altogether valueless. It can be approached only from the south, and after entering it there is nothing to do but leave. Ours has been the first, and will doubtless be the last, party of whites to visit this profitless locality."

Today Grand Canyon, Hoover Dam, and nearby Las Vegas attract over 50 million visitors each year.

JOHN WESLEY POWELL

IN 1848, FOLLOWING the Mexican-American War, the United States acquired the vast chunk of land that would one day make up California, Nevada, Arizona, Utah, Colorado, and New Mexico. But even by the 1860s, maps of the United States had a single word splashed across the Grand Canyon region: UNEXPLORED. Most men, even the heroically rugged trappers who opened up much of the West, took one look at those maps and stayed away. But one man looked at the maps and saw an opportunity for glory.

John Wesley Powell was probably the least likely man in America to conquer the Colorado River in Grand Canyon. A one-armed college professor with virtually no whitewater experience, he was a case study in everything that *wasn't* needed to navigate the river. At five feet, six inches tall, he hardly cut an imposing figure. But what Powell lacked in physical stature he more than made up for in personal ambition.

In 1868 Powell decided to organize an expedition to explore the Colorado River and the desolate canyon country it flowed through. He went to Washington, D.C., to raise money for the trip, but with the federal treasury still reeling from the Civil War, government funds were hard to come by. Powell was offered some military rations, however, which he gladly accepted. Undaunted, he scraped together funding from a variety of private institutions.

Powell's next step was to assemble a crew. The job offered life-threatening risks, harsh living conditions, and no pay. Not surprisingly, the men who accepted these terms were reckless, crazy, or a little of both. Most were trappers and mountain men eager for adventure and excitement. But to Powell, the journey was primarily a scientific expedition. "The object," he wrote, "is to make collections in geology, natural history, antiquities, and ethnology."

On May 24, 1869, Powell's expedition launched four boats from Green River City, Wyoming. Their starting point was 6,100 feet above sea level. Their destination, Grand Wash Cliffs near present-day Lake Mead, lay at an elevation of 1,300 feet. Exactly how the river got there was anyone's guess.

For the first week of their journey, the men floated peacefully down the Green River. The one-armed Powell, unable to row, sat perched on a chair tied to his boat. Some of the men were bored by the lazy current, but the river soon started to intensify. As they continued downstream, the rapids became frequent and fierce. Then on June 9, one of the boats slipped into a large rapid before the crew had a chance to scout it. The boat plunged into whitewater and smashed against a rock, splintering into pieces. The three men onboard swam to safety, but a third of the expedition's supplies were lost.

Following Disaster Falls (as Powell later named it) a nervous energy settled over the crew. They were only two weeks into their journey, and they had already lost one of their boats. What would happen if they lost another? The rapids were growing worse, and soon they would be hundreds of miles from civilization.

Determined, the men carried on. For the next two months they followed the Green River as it passed through Wyoming and Utah. They ran rapids whenever they could, but spent most of their time lining or portaging. Lining involved guiding the boats downstream as the men held ropes from shore. It was excruciating work. The ropes burned their hands and they were constantly slipping on wet rocks. The alternative was portaging, which entailed carrying the boats—and several thousand pounds of supplies—around the rapid.

By the time the expedition reached the confluence of the Green River and the Grand River, which marked the official start of the Colorado River, supplies were running low. They were down to several pounds of spoiled bacon, a few sacks of flour, and some dried apples. The men tried to supplement their diet by hunting, but game was scarce. Before long, the constant hunger and backbreaking days took a serious toll on group morale.

On August 4 the expedition reached the start of Grand Canyon. Drifting through its upper reaches, Powell was spellbound by the beautiful rock layers. He thought the highly polished limestone looked like marble, so he named the initial stretch Marble Canyon. The cliffs soon rose thousands of feet on either side. The scale of the canyon was breathtaking. "We are three quarters of a mile in the depths of the Earth," Powell wrote, "and the great river shrinks into insig-

Rescue by
UNDERWEAR!

In Desolation Canyon, Powell and a crew member named George Bradley set out to climb the steep cliffs above the river. As the one-armed Powell neared the top, he became stranded on the edge of a cliff. "Standing on my toes my muscles began to tremble," he wrote. "If I lose my hold I shall fall to the bottom." Powell called to Bradley, who quickly appeared on a ledge above. With time running out, Bradley stripped off his long johns and lowered them down. They dangled behind Powell just out of reach. Taking a deep breath, Powell leaned back into space and grabbed at the long johns with his one good hand. Catching a pant leg, Powell held on for dear life while Bradley hauled him to safety.

nificance, as it dashes its angry waves against the walls and cliffs, that rise to the world above; they are but puny ripples, and we are but pygmies."

While Powell marveled at the scenery, many of his crew felt trapped. Grand Canyon was like a prison to them. Daytime highs topped 100°F and the rapids were frequent and fierce. Before long, many of Powell's crew began to openly regret their decision to come.

Continuing on, the expedition twisted deep into the heart of Grand Canyon. Soon they were fighting off rapids the size of three-story buildings. Even worse, they had no idea what to expect around each bend in the river. There were rumors of giant waterfalls in Grand Canyon, and if those rumors proved true the expedition would find itself trapped at the bottom of a mile-deep chasm. Physically and mentally, the men were starting to unwind. They were now down to starvation rations, and the threat of death was very real.

On August 27 the men camped above the worst rapid yet. Many in the group doubted they could run it and survive. That night at dinner, a man named Oramel Howland took Powell aside. Howland told Powell that he and two others were abandoning the expedition. They would take their chances climbing out of Grand Canyon, even though that decision carried equally lethal implications.

Powell respected their decision, but he was convinced the rapid could be run. And according to his calculations, the group was just 50 miles from the end of their journey. He spent all night trying to convince the men not to leave, but they had seen enough. They left the following morning. It was the last time anyone saw the three men alive.

Concentrating on the matter at hand, Powell studied the rapid. The river was hemmed in by steep cliffs, so there was no possibility of portaging. And other than a small section at the top of the rapid, lining was also out of the question. With a slimmed-down crew, the men abandoned one of the boats and lined the remaining two boats as far as they could. Then they swooped into the rapid.

HERO or LIAR?

JAMES WHITE

In 1867, two years before Powell's expedition, a raft was pulled from the Colorado River just below Grand Canyon. On board was a starving, sunburned, half-naked man named James White, who proceeded to tell a story so amazing it's still disputed to this day. White claimed to have spent the previous two weeks floating down the Colorado lashed to a raft, making him the first man to successfully run Grand Canyon. Most modern scholars dispute White's story, based mostly on the fact that it's so hard to believe. But supposing it's true, White's journey would have been one of the most remarkable whitewater adventures of all time.

The first boat rushed down a steep wave and swamped with water. The men rowed for their lives. Soon the waves grew too large to do anything but hold on for dear life. The boats tossed and turned but somehow stayed upright. Before the men knew it, the rapid was behind them. Both boats had survived.

Two days later, Powell's expedition reached the end of its journey. As they approached the confluence of the Colorado River and the Virgin River, the men saw several Mormons fishing in the river. The Mormons had been posted there for weeks, under orders from Brigham Young to keep their eyes out "for any fragments or relics of [Powell's] party that might drift down the stream." They were shocked to see Powell and his men alive.

The hearts of the skeletal river runners were filled with joy. The Mormons cooked them a meal, and as one crew member recalled, "we laid our dignified manners aside and assumed the manner of so many hogs. Ate as long as we could and went to sleep to wake up hungry." After 99 days on the river, their voyage was finally over.

Powell's death-defying expedition is virtually impossible to imagine today. River guides who have spent decades rowing the modern, dam-controlled Colorado simply shake their heads in amazement when asked about Powell's journey. His under-supplied, ragtag collection of mountain men conquered the wildest, most unpredictable river in North America. Today their journey is often referred to as the last great expedition of the American West.

John Wesley Powell

JOHN WESLEY POWELL'S Colorado River expedition was one of the greatest adventures in American history. But nearly as remarkable as the expedition is the man who led it.

John Wesley Powell was born in 1834, the son of a poor itinerant preacher who moved his family across the frontier. As a young man Powell was constantly on the go, enrolling in several colleges but never staying long enough to graduate from any of them. When the Civil War broke out, Powell enlisted on the Union side, making lieutenant within his first two months. At the battle of Shiloh he was shot in his right arm—an injury that required amputation. Refusing to be kept out of the fight, Powell returned to battle several months later and accompanied General Sherman on his conquest of Georgia.

Following the war, Powell underwent an operation to ease the constant pain in his amputated arm. The operation failed, and for the rest of his life Powell was plagued with chronic pain from raw nerve endings at the end of his stump. Not one to dwell on personal misfortune, Powell simply looked to the future as he tried to figure out what to do with his life. "You are a maimed man," his father told him, "Settle down at teaching. It is a noble profession. Get this nonsense of science and adventure out of your mind."

Powell tried to settle down, but the lure of the West proved too powerful. As a geologist he led research trips to the headwaters of the Colorado and Green Rivers, whose waters ultimately flow through Grand Canyon. It was there that Powell developed an obsession with the Southwest. Powell the geologist was convinced the canyons of the Colorado River would show "the best geological section on the continent." Powell the adventurer desperately wanted to be the first to conquer the final frontier of the United States.

And conquer it he did. Following his Grand Canyon expedition, Powell spoke to packed lecture houses and stayed in the finest hotels. He used his influence to help found the Bureau of American Ethnology, the U.S. Geological Survey, and the National Geographic Society.

John Wesley Powell died in 1902. Shortly before his death, he made an unusual bet with his friend W.J. McGee, president of the National Geographic Society. Although physically smaller than McGee, Powell was convinced his brain was larger. To settle the dispute, the men left instructions to have their brains weighed following their deaths. At 1,488 grams, Powell's brain was five percent heavier. Today it rests in a jar at the Smithsonian Institution.

Bill Bass

EARLY SETTLERS

JOHN WESLEY POWELL'S journey inaugurated a wave of expeditions to map and explore Grand Canyon. Leading this charge was Powell himself. Shortly after his near-death, near-mutiny expedition, Powell announced plans to lead a second trip down the Colorado River. Many of his scientific notes had been lost on the first journey, and he was determined to fill in the blanks. This time, however, he would break his trip into stages with supply points along the way, thus reducing the risks involved. And so in 1871, the indefatigable Powell conquered the Colorado River again.

Between river trips Powell conducted scientific expeditions along the rim. But these excursions were temporary, and the region as a whole remained largely uninhabited by white settlers. Following the arrival of the railroad in northern Arizona in the early 1880s, however, a handful of drifters started taking up residence along the South Rim.

Most of the South Rim's early settlers were miners dreaming of riches in the depths of Grand Canyon. Although a number of potential mining sites were located, the costs of excavation proved prohibitively expensive. Ore had to be packed out on burros, water was scarce, and the closest railroad was two days away. Mining Grand Canyon, it tuned out, was an extremely unprofitable endeavor. But just as that realization started to sink in, the miners discovered an even better source of revenue: tourists.

Starting in the mid-1880s, people began arriving at Grand Canyon for no other reason than to visit, relax, and take in the views. This was a strikingly new concept. For hundreds of years, Grand Canyon had been avoided—even detested—as a destination. Now, people thought it was beautiful. This radical shift in perception would only grow in the years to come.

The first tourists arrived at the South Rim in 1884 and stayed in makeshift lodges built by miners. Most visitors arrived by stagecoach from the nearby towns of Flagstaff, Williams, and Ash Fork. But the journey was a rugged one. The dirt roads were filled with potholes, and the trip often required at least two days of bone-jarring travel.

It wasn't long before people started looking for a better form of transportation to the South Rim. In 1885 Grand Canyon entrepreneur Bill Bass lured a railroad agent to his lodge to try to convince him of the canyon's potential. The agent wasn't impressed. "No one," he wrote to his superiors, "would go that far only to see a hole in the ground."

It took over a decade for the railroads to realize their mistake. When they did, the previously isolated Grand Canyon became directly linked to the modern world—and visitors arrived by the thousands.

JOHN HANCE

JOHN HANCE was the first permanent white settler in Grand Canyon. After visiting on a prospecting trip in 1881, he fell in love with the scenery. Two years later he built a log cabin east of Grandview Point and rented out rooms to guests.

Hance is fondly remembered as Grand Canyon's premier storyteller, but his stories rarely contained a shred of truth. He took great pleasure in spinning tall tales with a deadpan delivery until his hapless listeners realized they'd been had. When Hance was asked how Grand Canyon formed, he responded, "It was hard work, took a long time, but I dug it myself, with a pick and a shovel. If you want to know what I done with the dirt, just look south through a clearin' in the trees at what they call the San Francisco Peaks." He also claimed to have jumped across Grand Canyon on horseback. Hance had hundreds of stories in his repertoire, and he never told the same story the same way twice.

As Hance once confided to a friend, "I've got to tell stories to them people for their money; and if I don't tell it to them, who will? I can make these tenderfeet believe that a frog eats boiled eggs; and I'm going to do it; and I'm going to make 'em believe that he carries it a mile to find a rock to crack it on."

The tenderfeet loved it. According to one early visitor, "Anyone who comes to the Grand Canyon and fails to meet John Hance will miss half the show." In 1906 he was offered free room and board at the Bright Angel Lodge in exchange for just hanging out with guests and being himself.

THE RAILROAD ARRIVES

MINERS AT THE rim weren't the only ones interested in a railroad to Grand Canyon. The nearby towns of Flagstaff and Williams also realized the benefits a railroad would bring—namely a steady flow of tourist dollars—and both towns were soon engaged in a feverish competition to build one. Flagstaff envisioned a railroad supported by tourism. The town's leading citizens pitched the idea to railroads, but, as Bill Bass had already discovered, railroads failed to grasp Grand Canyon's tourism potential.

Williams took a different approach. The town appealed to mining companies who needed a cheap way to haul ore from their mines near the South Rim. The new railroad would earn most of its profit from mining operations, with tourist dollars providing additional revenue. It was a shrewd pitch, and in 1897 the Santa Fe and Grand Canyon Railway Company was incorporated to build a railroad connecting Williams to the South Rim.

Four years later, the railroad reached Grand Canyon Village. By that time, however, the mines that prompted its construction had shut down. It hardly mattered. For $3.95 passengers could enjoy a smooth, four-hour train ride to the South Rim instead of a $20, bouncing, all-day stage ride, which was previously the only option. The result was predictable: tourism boomed.

Visitors arrived by the thousands. The railroad flourished, and before long the price of land near Grand Canyon Village skyrocketed. A few cunning locals staked bogus mining claims along the South Rim, giving them the questionable right to develop the land. Although the practice was ultimately ruled illegal, a few citizens—most notably Ralph Cameron (p.92)—became rich off the scheme.

The Santa Fe Railroad owned most of the land surrounding its tracks, giving it a strategic advantage in the real estate game. To accommodate the flood of new visitors, the Santa Fe Railroad built the extravagant El Tovar hotel in Grand Canyon Village. Early settlers who built hotels outside of Grand Canyon Village soon found it hard to compete with the new hotel. In little more than a decade, most locally owned hotels shut down.

Life on the South Rim was changing fast. Just three months after the first train pulled up, the first automobile arrived. Its driver departed from Flagstaff several days earlier amid much fanfare, but the car broke down shortly after it left. Several days later, the automobile arrived at the South Rim pulled by a team of mules. Within three decades, however, automobiles had become the most popular form of transportation to Grand Canyon, ultimately forcing the railroad out of business.

While the South Rim buzzed with tourist activity, the North Rim remained remote and isolated. No railroads came within 100 miles of the North Rim, and settlement in the region was scare. Because of its extreme isolation, the narrow strip of land between Grand Canyon and Utah, called the Arizona Strip, was a lawless area that attracted a strange mix of cattle thieves, renegades, and polygamist Mormons. Although Utah tried several times to annex the Arizona Strip, citing Arizona's poor law enforcement, Arizona was always able to retain control of the land.

Due to its remote location, the North Rim was filled with wild game, which eventually attracted hunting parties. North Rim sport hunting got off to a rocky start when a man named John Young tried to build a hunting lodge catering to British aristocrats. Young contacted Buffalo Bill Cody, who was then performing in England, and convinced him to round up a group of potential investors. When the wealthy Britons arrived later that year, they took one look at the desolate landscape and hightailed it back to England.

American hunters, on the other hand, were more than happy to venture to the rugged North Rim, where sport hunting soon flourished. In 1906 Congress established Grand Canyon Game Reserve, which included much of the North Rim. A few years later, ex-President Theodore Roosevelt visited the North Rim on a hunting trip. Starting from the South Rim, he descended the Bright Angel Trail to the Colorado River, then boarded a metal cage connected to a cable and pulley system. Halfway across the river, one of the cables snapped. The cage jolted violently, but Roosevelt made it safely across. After exiting the cage, the ever-exuberant Roosevelt cried out, "Let's do it again!"

Roosevelt's visit brought even greater attention to the region. It soon became clear that Grand Canyon was far more than a tourist attraction—it was a major national landmark. Many felt it deserved to be recognized as such. Before long, the wheels were in motion to create Grand Canyon National Park.

The South Rim
SWINDLER

Of ALL THE real estate swindlers who came to Grand Canyon in the late 1800s, none was more successful than Ralph Cameron. Shortly after the railroad arrived in 1901, Cameron began staking mining claims along the South Rim. Before long, he had claimed over 13,000 acres. But Cameron wasn't interested in mining. The claims gave him the right to develop the land, which was far more valuable as commercial real estate.

For his claims to be legal, however, Cameron needed to actually mine the land. He paid little attention to that technicality. Cameron simply "salted" the claims with imported minerals and set up bogus mining equipment. Once his claims were established, Cameron took great pleasure in lording them over the Santa Fe Railroad, which felt *it* had the right to develop the land.

One of Cameron's most contentious claims was located next to the Santa Fe Train Depot, a spot where he knew the railroad wanted to build a hotel. Cameron built his own hotel there instead. In retaliation, the railroad moved its terminal several hundred feet east so passengers would have to pass the railroad-owned Bright Angel Hotel on their way to Cameron's hotel. Visitation to Cameron's hotel plummeted.

But Cameron had one more trick up his sleeve. His "mining" claims also gave him sole control of the Bright Angel Trail, the only trail into Grand Canyon anywhere near Grand Canyon Village. Acting as tollkeeper, Cameron charged $1 for every tourist who descended the trail on horseback. The railroad filed a lawsuit, but Cameron prevailed in court. In retaliation, the railroad spent thousands of dollars improving the Hermit Trail, located several miles west of Grand Canyon Village, as an alternative to the Bright Angel Trail. Cameron, who also owned mining claims on the Hermit Trail, howled at the injustice. Tired of his antics, the railroad relented and paid him $40,000 for his bogus mining claims.

As the years wore on, Cameron lost the will to compete with the railroad. In 1910 he shut down his hotel, but he continued to charge a toll on the Bright Angel Trail. By the time the National Park Service finally gained control of the trail, Cameron had leveraged his wealth to become a U.S. senator, and for years he fought the park over the legitimacy of his mining claims. It wasn't until 1920 that the Arizona Supreme Court finally invalidated Cameron's mining claims, ending his once-grand real estate empire.

GRAND CANYON NATIONAL PARK

AS EARLY AS 1882, Indiana Senator Benjamin Harrison introduced legislation to create Grand Canyon National Park. At the time there was just one other national park, Yellowstone, which had been created a decade earlier. But Harrison's legislation faltered in the face of opposition from Arizona miners and ranchers. Harrison reintroduced legislation in 1883 and 1886, but again it failed. Two decades later, when Harrison became president, he used his power to establish "Great Canyon Reserve." It was a victory for Grand Canyon, but local miners and ranchers resented the new federal restrictions placed on the land.

Despite scattered local opposition, there were many people who agreed that Grand Canyon deserved protection. In 1906 President Theodore Roosevelt created Grand Canyon Game Reserve on the North Rim. It was an easy decision for Roosevelt. He had visited Grand Canyon a few years earlier and proclaimed it "the most impressive scenery I have ever looked at."

The creation of Grand Canyon Game Reserve was just the beginning. Two years later, Roosevelt used the new powers granted to him by the Antiquities Act to establish Grand Canyon National Monument. A national park required an act of Congress, but the Antiquities Act let presidents declare national monuments for areas that held "objects of historic or scientific nature."

At the time, Arizona was not yet a state, so it had no senators or congressmen to champion the creation of a national park. Arizona was admitted to the Union in 1912, and five years late Representative Carl Hayden and Senator Henry Fountain introduced legislation to create Grand Canyon National Park. On February 26, 1919, President Woodrow Wilson signed the bill into law.

But creating a national park and running it were two different matters. Early administrators lacked a coherent vision for the park, and many major issues went unresolved. In its first decade of operation, Grand Canyon National Park went through six superintendents. The park needed a strong leader with long-term vision, and it found that leader in Miner Tillotson, a civil engineer who became superintendent in 1927. Tillotson served as superintendent for over a decade, shaping a coherent vision for years to come.

The same year that Tillotson became superintendent, Congress revised the park's boundaries to include a large portion of Kaibab National Forest. Five years later, President Herbert Hoover proclaimed a new Grand Canyon National Monument (the old one had become Grand Canyon National Park) that encompassed 300 square miles in western Grand Canyon and an additional 40 miles along the Colorado River.

The park was a success on paper, but a flood of new visitors overwhelmed the staff. In its first year as a national park, Grand Canyon received 44,000 visitors. Within a decade, that number rose to nearly 200,000. In 1937, 300,000 people arrived. The numbers kept on climbing, but the park's staff remained the same: ten rangers and one park superintendent. For years a small, dedicated staff worked long hours to accommodate the huge number of visitors. Eventually the number of rangers increased, making Grand Canyon National Park much more enjoyable for both tourists and rangers alike.

THE GREAT DAM WARS

BY THE 1960s, Grand Canyon seemed to be doing just fine. Its dedicated staff welcomed millions of visitors from around the world. Movie stars, British royalty, Arab sheiks, and Albert Einstein all stopped by for a look. The giant hole in the ground that had been avoided for centuries was now one of America's most cherished natural landmarks. Best of all, Grand Canyon's national park status protected it from private development. But a massive government project soon threatened to drastically alter the landscape.

In the early 1960s, the U.S. Bureau of Reclamation (the government agency responsible for much of the West's water supply) went looking for a new place to build a dam. Ever since the massive success of Hoover Dam, the Bureau of Reclamation had been constructing giant dams at a frantic rate. The West was growing fast, and it needed water to grow. In the 1930s, '40s, and '50s, the

HARPER'S
WEEKLY

EDITED BY GEORGE HARVEY

W.H.D.Koerner·11

Bureau of Reclamation built dams wherever it could. Before long, many of the Southwest's most powerful and impressive rivers resembled a string of interconnected reservoirs. By the 1960s, there was only one good place left to build a giant dam in the West: Grand Canyon.

With its steep walls, deep side canyons, and powerful river, Grand Canyon was perfect for an enormous dam. But there was a catch: any reservoir created by a dam would be totally impractical from a water-use standpoint. Because water from the reservoir would need to be pumped out thousands of feet to bring it to civilization, the costs involved would be prohibitively expensive. But the Bureau of Reclamation wasn't interested in water. It was interested in hydroelectricity. In effect, a giant dam in Grand Canyon would be nothing more than a giant cash register to fund other, less economically feasible water projects elsewhere. And the Bureau of Reclamation didn't just want one giant dam in Grand Canyon—it wanted *two.*

When conservationists heard the news, they went wild. Conservationists hate dams, a fact that became apparent in 1948 when the Bureau of Reclamation tried to build a dam along the Green River in Echo Park, Utah. The dam would have flooded part of Dinosaur National Monument, and conservationists were loath to let that happen. Led by David Brower of the Sierra Club, conservationists fought tooth and nail to defeat the dam. Although they succeeded, that success came at an enormous cost.

As part of the compromise to save Dinosaur National Monument, the two sides agreed upon a new dam farther downstream at Glen Canyon. Lying just north of Grand Canyon, Glen Canyon was one of the most remote places in the country. Only a few thousand people had ever seen it. So shortly before Glen Canyon Dam was finished, David Brower, the man who inadvertently championed its creation, took a river trip through Glen Canyon to see the landscape firsthand. He immediately started to cry.

With its gorgeous sandstone arches, fern covered alcoves, and sweeping river views, Glen Canyon was one of the most beautiful places Brower had ever seen. In a few months, it would lie beneath Lake Powell. Brower later admitted that

FLOYD DOMINY

"**I** like Dave Brower, but I don't think he's the sanctified conservationist that so many people think he is. I think he's a selfish preservationist, for the few. Dave Brower hates my guts. Why? Because I've got guts. I've tangled with Dave Brower for many years."

the creation of Glen Canyon Dam was the greatest failure of his life. From that moment forward, he vowed never again to lose another beautiful place to a dam. When Brower found out the Bureau of Reclamation wanted to build *two* dams in Grand Canyon, he went into overdrive.

Brower was up against stiff competition. The biggest proponent of the Grand Canyon dams was Floyd Dominy, head of the Bureau of Reclamation. Dominy had spent much of his early career helping struggling Wyoming ranchers build dams that saved their families from poverty. He knew firsthand how a lack of water could lead to suffering, and he made it his life's mission to build dams. Dominy's drive and ambition were unprecedented. By the time he became head of the Bureau of Reclamation, he had many powerful allies, including Arizona Senator Carl Hayden, chairman of the Appropriations Committee.

Brower versus Dominy. Conservation versus economic growth. The battle over the Grand Canyon dams became much more than a battle over Grand Canyon. It became a battle over the future of environmental policy in America. For decades economic development had taken precedent over wilderness. But wilderness was disappearing fast, and many people wanted to preserve what was left before it was too late.

Debate over the Grand Canyon dams soon shifted into the public arena. Defending the proposed dams, the Bureau of Reclamation argued that the reservoirs would help tourists enjoy Grand Canyon by allowing them to explore previously inaccessible areas in motorboats. In response, the Sierra Club took out full-page ads in the *New York Times*, *Los Angeles Times*, *San Francisco Chronicle*, and *Washington Post* that read: "Should we also flood the Sistine Chapel so tourists can get nearer the ceiling?"

The response was overwhelming. Letters protesting the dams arrived at the Bureau of Reclamation in dump trucks. Senators and congressmen were flooded with requests to save Grand Canyon. The two dams, which would have flooded much of Marble Canyon and Lower Granite Gorge—including Havasu Canyon, one of the most beautiful side canyons in Grand Canyon—were stopped dead in their tracks.

DAVID BROWER

"Lake Powell is a drag strip for power boats. It's for people who won't do things except the easy way. The magic of Glen Canyon is dead. It has been vulgarized. Putting water in the Cathedral in the Desert was like urinating on the crypt of St. Peter's."

GRAND CANYON TODAY

TODAY THE BIGGEST challenge facing Grand Canyon National Park is visitation. In 1956 one million people visited Grand Canyon. Thirteen years later, that number doubled. Twenty years later it tripled. To cope with increased traffic and pollution, the park service closed Hermit Road to private vehicles in 1974 and offered a free shuttle instead. To deal with overcrowding below the rim, the park instituted a permit and reservation system for overnight camping. Before the permit system, it was not unusual for hundreds of people to camp near Phantom Ranch at the bottom of Grand Canyon, a place that can comfortably accommodate about 90 people.

To cope with increased visitation in the future, the National Park Service drafted a General Management Plan to reduce human impact on the park and keep Grand Canyon in as natural a state as possible. Under the plan, which will be instituted over time, private cars will not be allowed over much of the South Rim and visitors will be shuttled around entirely by bus or a proposed light rail system. Extensive "Greenway Trails" have also been built along the rim for bikers and pedestrians.

Today over six million people visit Grand Canyon each year. Those numbers are both a blessing and a challenge. But as long as every visitor makes a conscious effort to appreciate and preserve Grand Canyon, it will remain one of the world's great destinations for generations to come.

FLAGSTAFF REGION

Grand Canyon Village

Desert View

Tusayan

64

89

180

San Francisco Peaks

Wupatki

Flagstaff

Sunset Crater

40

Williams

Walnut Canyon

40

Sedona

17

Meteor Crater

FLAGSTAFF REGION

F LAGSTAFF IS THE largest town (population 70,000) in northern Arizona and a popular jumping-off point for visitors heading to Grand Canyon's South Rim. Situated at the base of the tallest mountains in Arizona, the San Francisco Peaks, Flagstaff has a historic downtown filled with hotels and restaurants. The 74-mile drive from Flagstaff to the South Rim is roughly one hour and 20 minutes.

Williams, Arizona, located 34 miles west of Flagstaff, is a much smaller town (population 3,000), but there are plenty of hotels and restaurants catering to Grand Canyon visitors. Located on historic Route 66 (p.300), the town's charming Main Street retains a classic 1950s vibe. The Grand Canyon Railway (p.116), which makes daily trips to the South Rim, departs from the town's historic train depot. The 54-mile drive from Williams to the South Rim is about one hour.

The tiny town of Tusayan (population 583), located just one mile south of Grand Canyon's South Entrance Station, revolves entirely around Grand Canyon tourism. Tusayan has a small airport south of town, and its main street is lined with hotels and restaurants.

Grand Canyon steals the show in northern Arizona, but the Flagstaff region has some great, overlooked national monuments. Wupatki National Monument (p.106) features some of Arizona's most dramatic archaeological ruins. Walnut Canyon National Monument (p.106) is another interesting archaeological site that's delightfully crowd-free. Just north of Flagstaff, Sunset Crater National Monument (p.107) features northern Arizona's youngest volcano, which erupted 900 years ago.

If you're interested in astronomy and space, the Flagstaff region also has plenty to offer. Start your journey at the Lowell Observatory (p.103), where Pluto was discovered in 1930. Even if you're not interested in astronomy, the observatory's beautiful grounds are worth a visit. Another great destination is Meteor Crater (p.107), located roughly 40 miles southeast of Flagstaff. Blasted out by a meteor that hit northern Arizona roughly 50,000 years ago, it's one of the best preserved meteor impact craters in the world.

Visit jameskaiser.com for lodging recommendations in Flagstaff and Williams

Flagstaff

This big little town is the unofficial capital of northern Arizona. It's home to Northern Arizona University, whose 30,000 students give Flagstaff a young, outdoorsy vibe. While the outskirts of town feature chain restaurants and big box retailers, the historic downtown is filled with local shops, bistros, and breweries. The Museum of Northern Arizona (musnaz.org) is a great place to learn about the region's natural and cultural history. And Flagstaff's dark, starry skies are a magnet for astronomers, who work at both the Lowell Observatory and the U.S. Naval Observatory. In 2001 Flagstaff was declared the world's first International Dark Sky City thanks to its efforts to reduce light pollution.

Flagstaff was settled in 1876 and named after a ponderosa pine flagpole used by early residents. The name is appropriate. Flagstaff is surrounded by the largest contiguous ponderosa forest in the country, and lumber was one of the town's most important early industries. The first railroad arrived in 1882, and by 1886 Flagstaff was the largest town between Albuquerque and the West Coast. The town got a further boost when Route 66 passed through in 1926.

Flagstaff is located at an elevation of 6,900 feet. Just north of town are the San Francisco Peaks, which rise nearly 6,000 feet above town. The Arizona Snow Bowl offers downhill skiing in winter (arizonasnowbowl.com), and there's great hiking in spring, summer, and fall. In mid-October, when the foliage peaks, the San Francisco Peaks shimmer with golden aspen trees.

Lowell Observatory

Perched on Mars Hill, which offers great views of Flagstaff and the San Francisco Peaks, Lowell Observatory is one of America's most charming and historic observatories. It was built in 1894 by Percival Lowell, heir to a Boston fortune, who became obsessed with finding life on Mars. Flagstaff boasts some of the best stargazing conditions in the country thanks to its high elevation and dry climate, so Lowell moved west and built an observatory here. After it was operational, Lowell spent the next two decades looking for evidence of life on Mars. He also postulated the existence of "Planet X," a hypothetical planet beyond Neptune.

Lowell died in 1916, having failed to find either Planet X or life on Mars. Thirteen years later, a 23-year-old self-taught astronomer named Clyde Tombaugh arrived at the Lowell Observatory. Working long hours for little pay, Tombaugh diligently took photos of the night sky. In 1930, while reviewing the photos, he found evidence of Planet X. The discovery of a new planet by a self-taught 24-year-old sent shock waves around the world. Planet X was named Pluto after the Roman god of the underworld, who could render himself invisible. Although Pluto was ultimately downgraded to "dwarf planet" in 2006, its discovery remains one of the seminal moments in American astronomy.

Tours of the Lowell Observatory are offered daily, and there's a terrific museum and gift shop. Open 10am–10pm Mon–Sat, 10am–5pm Sunday (1400 West Mars Hill Road, 928-774-3358, lowell.edu).

San Francisco Peaks

Just north of Flagstaff lie the tallest mountains in Arizona, the San Francisco Peaks. Rising 12,633 feet above sea level, the mountains are considered sacred by several native tribes, including the Hopi, who believe spirit beings called Kachinas live among the peaks they call *Nuva'tukya'ovi* ("Place of Snow on Top"). The Navajo, who call the peaks *Dook'o'oosłííd* ("Summit Which Never Melts"), consider it the Sacred Mountain of the West. The San Francisco Peaks are remnants of an ancient volcano that once towered 16,000 feet above sea level—taller than any current mountain between Mexico and Canada. Around 200,000 years ago the volcano erupted, blasting off 4,000 feet of mountaintop and leaving behind the current peaks. The San Francisco Peaks are the largest ancient volcano in the San Francisco Volcanic Field, an 1,800-square-mile region where over 600 volcanoes have erupted. For nearly six million years—roughly the same age as Grand Canyon—these volcanoes have spewed nearly 120 cubic miles of lava over northern Arizona. Without the volcanoes, the region between Flagstaff and Grand Canyon would be a mostly flat plain. Instead, it's pockmarked with hills and mountains. Geologists believe this volcanically active region is located above a "hot spot" where lava rises up from deep within earth's mantle. The most recent volcanic eruption was 900 years ago at Sunset Crater (p.107), and future eruptions are all but inevitable. Fortunately, most historic eruptions have been relatively non-explosive—more like the slow-motion eruptions on Hawaii than a sudden, massive explosion like Mount St. Helens.

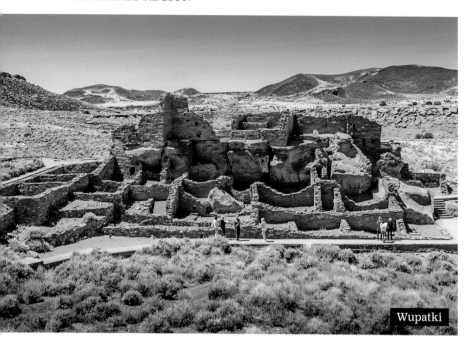

Wupatki

Wupatki

Located six miles northeast of Flagstaff, Wupatki showcases the most impressive archaeological ruins in northern Arizona. The large stone buildings were constructed around A.D. 1100, when roughly 2,000 Ancestral Puebloans migrated here to farm beans, corn, and squash. What triggered this sudden influx is a mystery. It may have been related to the eruption of nearby Sunset Crater, which blanketed the region with ash that improved agricultural productivity. For a brief time, the new arrivals flourished, building multi-story structures out of blocks of local sandstone. The largest structure, Wupatki, which means "Tall House" in the Hopi language, contained 100 rooms, including a nearby community center and ballcourt. At its peak, as many as 100 people may have lived in Wupatki, which sat at the crossroads of a vibrant trading network. Then, around A.D. 1225, the region was suddenly abandoned for unknown reasons. Open 9am–5pm.

Walnut Canyon

Located ten miles southeast of Flagstaff, this remote canyon is home to dozens of ancient cliff dwellings. It was occupied by the Sinagua people for nearly 150 years between A.D. 1100 and 1250. A one-mile trail descends halfway down the 400-foot canyon, passing 25 stone dwellings along the way. Though not as dramatic as the famous cliff dwellings at Mesa Verde or Canyon de Chelly, Walnut Canyon is definitely worth a visit. Open 9am–5pm.

Meteor Crater

Sunset Crater

This large cinder cone, located 12 miles north of Flagstaff, is an uncomfortable reminder that northern Arizona is still volcanically active. Sunset Crater erupted 900 years ago—which, geologically speaking, is the blink of an eye. Lava flows from the eruption extended six miles, and ash blanketed 800 square miles. As the name implies, Sunset Crater is lovely at sunset, but sunrise is also beautiful. Sunset Crater is a national monument, and the visitor center is filled with displays explaining its fascinating geology. You can't climb the crater, but several easy hiking trails pass ancient lava flows. Open 9am–5pm.

Meteor Crater

Roughly 50,000 years ago, a 160-foot meteor traveling 26,000 miles per hour struck northern Arizona. The blast was equivalent to a ten-megaton bomb. When the dust settled, an impact crater 4,000 feet wide was left behind. Today Meteor Crater, located 40 miles east of Flagstaff, is one of the best-preserved meteor impact craters in world. In the 1960s NASA astronauts trained in the crater to prepare for the Apollo mission to the moon. Although Meteor Crater is located on private property, it's operated as a tourist attraction open to the public. A large visitor center offers exhibits and a short movie, but the real highlight is visiting the observation platforms on the crater's rim. Open 7am–7pm in summer 8am–5pm the rest of the year (meteorcrater.com).

TUSAYAN

This tiny town is located just south of Grand Canyon's South Entrance Station. Sandwiched between Grand Canyon to the north and Kaibab National Forest to the south, Tusayan is the only private property anywhere near Grand Canyon Village. Its commercial district, which lines both sides of AZ-64, is filled with hotels, restaurants, and the area's only gas station. Grand Canyon Airport, located just south of town, offers scenic airplane and helicopter flights.

From Tusayan to the Grand Canyon Visitor Center it's a roughly 15-minute drive. But during peak season (March to September) there are often traffic jams. Consider parking in Tusayan and riding the free shuttle to Grand Canyon Visitor Center. Another option is parking in Tusayan and biking 6.5 miles to the Grand Canyon Visitor Center along the paved Greenway Trail.

Lodging & Camping

Lodging in Tusayan is often more expensive than lodging in the park because many Tusayan hotels offer luxuries such as swimming pools and spas. But when park hotels are fully booked, Tusayan hotels are your next best bet. Camping options include the private Grand Canyon Camper Village and the public Ten X Campground in nearby Kaibab National Forest. For complete Tusayan lodging and camping info visit jameskaiser.com.

Dining

YIPPEI-EI-O! STEAKHOUSE $$$

This cowboy-themed restaurant serves steaks and ribs cooked over juniper wood, plus some vegetarian options. Try the rattlesnake appetizer (928-638-2780).

PLAZA BONITA $$$

If you're feeling like Mexican food, head to Plaza Bonita, which features all the classics: tacos, burritos, fajitas, enchiladas, chimichangas (928-638-4654).

CANYON STAR $$$

Located in the Grand Hotel, Canyon Star offers Southwestern fare (steaks, ribs) plus burgers, soups, salads. The bar has a large beer selection (928-638-3333).

CORONADO DINING ROOM $$$

Located in the Best Western, the menu is heavy on steakhouse favorites, including local specialties like elk (928-638-2681).

WE COOK PIZZA AND PASTA $$$

Serves—you guessed it—pizza and pasta (928-638-2278).

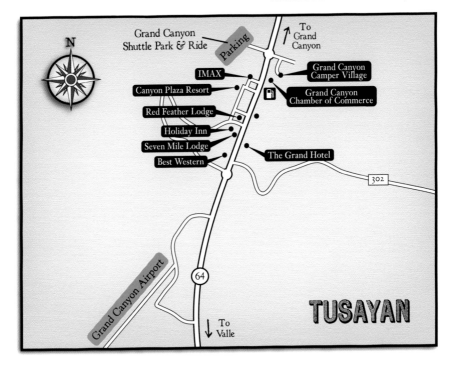

Entertainment

IMAX THEATER

Year after year, the IMAX film *Grand Canyon: The Hidden Secrets* lures visitors to its 70-foot screen. Short of going on a two-week river trip, this is a great way to check out some of Grand Canyon's most spectacular scenery. The 35-minute movie plays every hour on the half-hour (explorethecanyon.com).

APACHE STABLES

Located one mile north of Tusayan, Apache Stables offers one- and two-hour horseback rides through the Kaibab National Forest during the day and campfire wagon rides in the evening.(928-638-2891, apachestables.com).

Scenic Flights

Scenic airplane and helicopter flights depart daily from Grand Canyon Airport. Many people prefer helicopters, which offer a slower ride and lower elevations, but airplanes cover more ground in less time. Helicopter flights (25–50 minutes, $215–320 per person) are offered by Maverick (maverickhelicopter.com), Papillon (papillon.com), and Grand Canyon Helicopters (grandcanyonhelicopter.com). Airplane flights (45 minutes, $135–200 per person) are offered by Papillon, Grand Canyon Airlines (grandcanyonairlines.com) and Westwind Air Services (westwindairservice.com).

THE SOUTH RIM

STUNNING VIEWS, TERRIFYING depths, soaring condors—these are just a few of the things you'll find at the South Rim, the most famous and popular part of Grand Canyon National Park. Perched a mile above the Colorado River at one of Grand Canyon's widest points, the South Rim offers a fabulous introduction to earth's greatest geologic marvel.

Because of its proximity to Interstate 40, the South Rim is the most accessible—and crowded—part of the park. But no matter how crowded it gets, the views are always worth it. And if you follow the tips in this guide, it's easy to find peace and solitude, even during the busy summer months.

The South Rim has two entrances: South Entrance, just north of the town of Tusayan (p.108), and East Entrance, near Desert View (p.166). If possible, enter at East Entrance. You'll avoid peak season traffic jams at South Entrance and enjoy beautiful scenery along Desert View Drive. If you enter at South Entrance during peak season (March through September), try to arrive before 9am or after 5pm to avoid traffic. Or park in Tusayan and ride the free shuttle into the park.

The South Rim is divided into three main areas: Grand Canyon Village, Hermit Road, and Desert View Drive. Nearly all of the park's hotels, restaurants, and shops are clustered around Grand Canyon Village (elevation 6,800 feet). Its five lodges accommodate about 1,000 guests, and you can find everything from museums to gift shops to mule rides. To reduce traffic, the park offers free shuttles between popular points in Grand Canyon Village.

Hermit Road heads seven miles west of Grand Canyon Village to some of the park's most famous viewpoints. Although closed to private vehicles from March through November, you can still reach the viewpoints by hiking, biking, or riding the free Hermit Road shuttle. Desert View Drive, which is open to private vehicles year-round, heads 22 miles east from Grand Canyon Village to Desert View.

Hiking and biking are two of the best ways to explore the South Rim. The easy, 12.8-mile Rim Trail (p.119) skirts the edge of Grand Canyon between South Kaibab Trailhead and Hermits Rest, passing over a dozen jaw-dropping viewpoints along the way. For a more challenging hike, descend partway down the South Kaibab Trail (p.180), which has better views and fewer crowds than the more famous Bright Angel Trail (p.170). Bicyclists can enjoy any paved road along the rim (including Hermit Road), plus 15 miles of Greenway Trails built specifically for bikes. Bike rentals are available from Bright Angel Bicycles (p.25).

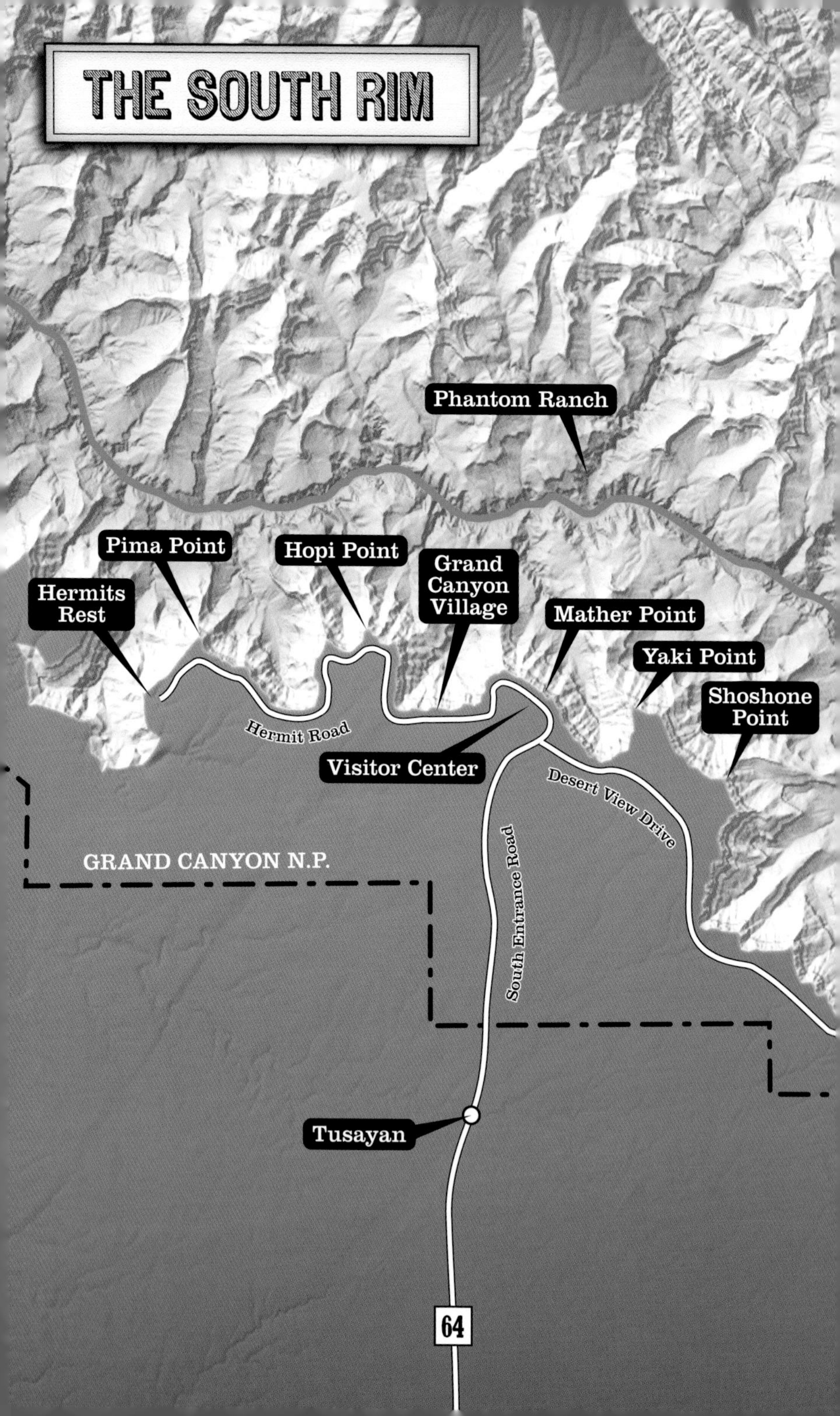

THE SOUTH RIM

Phantom Ranch

Pima Point

Hopi Point

Grand Canyon Village

Mather Point

Yaki Point

Hermits Rest

Shoshone Point

Hermit Road

Visitor Center

Desert View Drive

GRAND CANYON N.P.

South Entrance Road

Tusayan

64

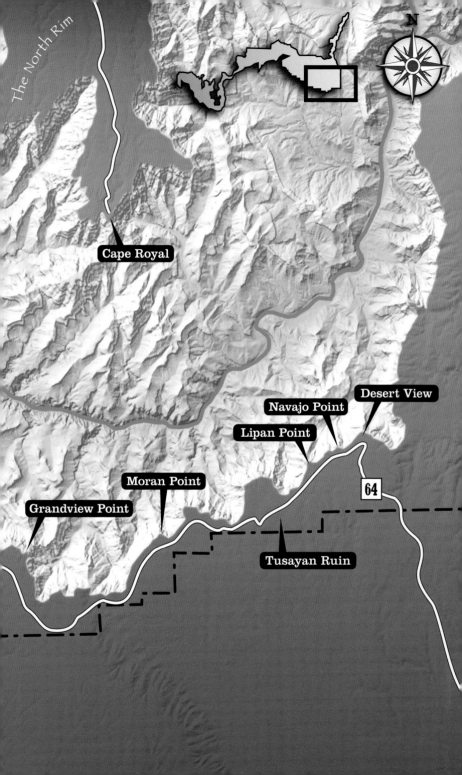

One Perfect Day
on the South Rim

After watching sunrise over earth's greatest natural wonder, have breakfast at Bright Angel Restaurant (p.114). Then catch the shuttle to Yavapai Point (p.128) and visit the Yavapai Geology Museum. Put your new geological knowledge to work on the 1.3-mile Trail of Time (p.129), which finishes near Verkamp's Visitor Center (p.129) and Hopi House (p.130). Next, catch the shuttle to Canyon Village Deli (p.122), pick up sandwiches to go, and head back to the rim for a picnic lunch. Afterwards, book an afternoon Hermit Road Tour with Bright Angel Bicycles (p.119). If you have time after the tour, look for free late afternoon ranger programs (p.111). Finally, pick a fabulous spot for sunset and top off your perfect day with dinner and drinks at El Tovar Hotel (p.132).

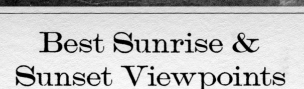

"At length, as the sun draws near the horizon, the great drama of the day begins . . . All things seem to grow in beauty, power, and dimensions. What was grand before has become majestic, the majestic becomes sublime, and, ever expanding and developing, the sublime passes beyond the reach of our faculties and becomes transcendent."

—Clarence Dutton, 1882

Best Sunrise & Sunset Viewpoints

Sunrise: Mather Point (p.127) is Grand Canyon's most famous sunrise viewpoint—but that's mostly because it's located next to the visitor center. Yaki Point (p.156) and Shoshone Point (p.157) have even better eastern views, but each require slightly more effort to get to. Other good options are Yavapai Point and Desert View (p.166).

Sunset: Hopi Point (p.146) is Grand Canyon's most famous sunset viewpoint, but you'll be sharing the view with dozens of tourists, and everyone wants to catch the shuttle back at the same time. Mohave Point (p.148) and Pima Point (p.150) are great alternatives. Yavapai Point has the best sunsets near Grand Canyon Village, and Desert View has beautiful western views.

Tip: No matter which viewpoint you choose on Hermit Road or Grand Canyon Village, walk a few minutes east or west along the Rim Trail. You'll find similar views with a fraction of the crowds.

South Rim
BASICS

Getting to the South Rim

BY CAR

Grand Canyon's South Entrance lies just north of the small town of Tusayan, which is about 50 miles north of Williams and 60 miles north of Flagstaff. Unfortunately, South Entrance traffic jams are common during peak season (March through September) with waits up to one hour. **Tip #1:** Arrive before 9am or after 5pm to avoid traffic. **Tip #2:** during peak season, South Entrance has a "fast lane" for cars with entrance permits, which you can buy in Tusayan at the Grand Canyon Chamber of Commerce.

East Entrance, located 25 miles east of Grand Canyon Village on Desert View Drive, is more remote and rarely suffers traffic jams. To get there drive 47 miles north of Flagstaff on US-89, then turn west onto AZ-64.

Note: the Grand Canyon Visitor Center parking area often fills up by 10am. If there's no space, continue to parking lots A, B, C or D in Grand Canyon Village.

BY BICYCLE

Avoid traffic jams altogether! Park in Tusayan and ride the paved, 6.5-mile Greenway Trail into Grand Canyon National Park.

BY SHUTTLE

From March through September, a free park shuttle runs daily trips between the town of Tusayan and the Grand Canyon Visitor Center. **Groome Transportation** (groometransportation.com) offers private shuttle service from Flagstaff and Williams to the South Rim. **Transcanyon Shuttle** (trans-canyonshuttle.com) offers daily shuttles between the South Rim and North Rim.

BY TRAIN

Grand Canyon Railway offers daily service between Williams and Grand Canyon Village. The trip is roughly two-hours, and they train arrives at 11:45am and departs at 3:30pm. Overnight packages are available. (thetrain.com)

BY PLANE

The two closest major airports are **McCarran International Airport** in Las Vegas and **Phoenix Sky Harbor International Airport**. Some airlines fly into **Pulliam Airport** in Flagstaff. Grand Canyon Airlines offers flights to **Grand Canyon Airport** in Tusayan from Boulder City, Nevada, near Las Vegas.

Fees

A seven-day pass to the South Rim (which includes access to the North Rim) costs $35 per vehicle, $30 per motorcycle, or $20 per pedestrian or cyclist. There's also an annual Grand Canyon Pass ($70). The best deal, however, is America the Beautiful Pass ($80), which gives you unlimited access to all U.S. national parks, national monuments, and federal recreation lands for one year.

Information

You can download Grand Canyon's free *Trip Planner* at nps.gov/grca. A free South Rim Pocket Map, which lists basic info and current shuttle routes, is available online and at entrance stations, visitor centers, hotels, and campgrounds. Grand Canyon's Twitter feed (@GrandCanyonNPS) is a great resource for weather updates and park alerts.

The Grand Canyon Visitor Center (p.126) is the park's main visitor center. There are also ranger-staffed information desks at Yavapai Geology Museum (p.128), Verkamp's Visitor Center (p.129), Kolb Studio (p.139), Tusayan Museum (p.162), and Desert View (p.166).

Transportation desks at Bright Angel Lodge, Maswik Lodge, and Yavapai Lodge offer information on mule rides and motor tours. The South Rim's Backcountry Information Center, where backpackers can inquire about hiking permits and trail conditions, is located behind Maswik Lodge.

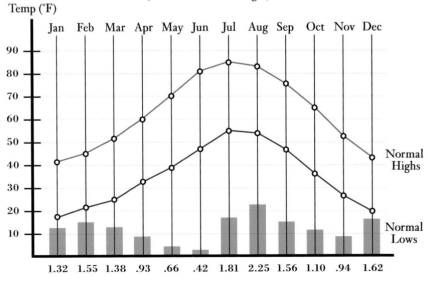

SOUTH RIM CLIMATE
(based on annual averages)

Temp (°F)

	Jan	Feb	Mar	Apr	May	Jun	Jul	Aug	Sep	Oct	Nov	Dec
Precipitation (inches)	1.32	1.55	1.38	.93	.66	.42	1.81	2.25	1.56	1.10	.94	1.62

Normal Highs

Normal Lows

Precipitation (inches)

Weather & When to Go

SPRING

Spring is one of the best times to visit the South Rim. Temperatures are mild, precipitation is light, and crowds are manageable. Early spring is also a great time to hike the South Rim's inner canyon trails, which become brutally hot in summer. By June daily highs on the South Rim can top 80°F. That said, snowfall has been recorded as late as mid-June! Spring is also wildflower season. The intensity of wildflower blooms depends on precipitation—some years the blooms are spectacular, other years they are far less dramatic.

SUMMER

Summer is the most popular time to visit Grand Canyon, but it's also the season of big crowds, hot temperatures, and late-summer thunderstorms. The view from the rim remains spectacular, however, and a thunderstorm over Grand Canyon is an amazing sight to behold. Thunderstorms, which generally occur in the afternoon, are most common during "monsoon season," which lasts from July through mid-September. Lightning is common during monsoon season. If you hear thunder, move away from the rim and seek shelter inside buildings or vehicles, *not* under trees. If the weather is clear and sunny, remember that scorching midday temperatures in the inner canyon make many of the park's popular hiking trails unbearable in July and August. Phantom Ranch, at the bottom of Grand Canyon, has recorded summer highs of 120°F!

FALL

Fall is a terrific time to visit Grand Canyon. The crowds drop off after Labor Day, and monsoons generally end around mid-September. As the days grow shorter, Grand Canyon is bathed in gorgeous autumn light. Like spring, fall is a great time to hike inner canyon trails due to milder temperatures. Fall weather can be unpredictable, however, so bring plenty of warm clothes and rain gear. By mid-October, nighttime temperatures often drop below freezing along the South Rim.

WINTER

Winter is the most underrated season at Grand Canyon. Daily highs hover in the 40s and temperatures drop below freezing at night. But winter also means minimal crowds, reduced rates at park lodges, and the possibility of snow. The South Rim averages about five feet of snow each winter. If you visit during or after a snowstorm, you'll witness Grand Canyon at its most beautiful. You'll need warm clothes on the rim, but the bottom of Grand Canyon often experiences spring-like temperatures in winter, making it a great time to spend the night at Phantom Ranch (p.179) or Bright Angel Campground (p.121). Note: the North Rim closes in winter due to heavy snow.

Getting Around the South Rim

BY CAR

Exploring the South Rim by car lets you hop from point to point at your own pace. Unfortunately, traffic and parking in Grand Canyon Village are anything but leisurely. Around Grand Canyon Village, it's far better to park your car and use the free shuttle system. Also be aware that the seven-mile Hermit Road is closed to private vehicles from March through November. For a beautiful scenic drive, check out the 22-mile Desert View Drive.

BY SHUTTLE

To help reduce traffic and pollution, the park offers free shuttles between popular destinations in Grand Canyon Village and along Hermit Road. A seasonal shuttle also runs between the town of Tusayan and Grand Canyon Visitor Center. The free South Rim Pocket Map lists seasonal shuttle routes and schedules.

BY BICYCLE

Biking is one of my favorite ways to explore the South Rim. Bicycles are permitted on paved roads, but vehicle traffic can be an issue during peak season. Fortunately, the South Rim has roughly 13 miles of Greenway Trails—paved roads designed specifically for bicycle riders. Greenway Trails radiate out from Grand Canyon Visitor Center to Grand Canyon Village, the South Kaibab Trail, and the nearby town of Tusayan. Bicyclists also enjoy privileged access to Hermit Road, which is closed to private vehicles from March through November. Three miles of Greenway Trails are also available along Hermit Road between Monument Creek Vista and Hermits Rest. All of the park's free shuttles are equipped with bicycle racks. Bike rentals and guided tours are available from Bright Angel Bicycles (928-814-8704, bikegrandcanyon.com), located at Grand Canyon Visitor Center. See page 25 for more biking info.

ON FOOT VIA THE RIM TRAIL

Hiking is one of the best ways to experience Grand Canyon, slowing down the pace so you can revel in the magnificent scenery. The easy, 12.8-mile Rim Trail skirts the canyon rim from Hermits Rest to South Kaibab Trailhead, passing the South Rim's most famous viewpoints. Free park shuttles service many of the viewpoints, so you can hike along the Rim Trail for as little or as long as you'd like, then catch the shuttle back. Although the Rim Trail is often crowded near popular viewpoints, long stretches in between offer plenty of peace and quiet. One gorgeous section, which most people overlook, is the four-mile stretch from Hopi Point to Pima Point. If you're interested in geology, check out the Trail of Time (p.129), a walking timeline of earth history stretching 2.8 miles between Yavapai Point and Verkamp's Visitor Center. The park also offers a free, ranger-led Rim View Walk during peak season.

Lodging

Most South Rim hotels are run by Xanterra (grandcanyonlodges.com). Yavapai Lodge is run by DNC (visitgrandcanyon.com). Rooms fill up fast, so book your reservations as far in advance as possible, especially for the busy summer months. Rates below are based on peak season. Winter rates are often cheaper. If no rooms are available in the park, check hotels in Tusayan (p.108).

★ EL TOVAR HOTEL

This historic hotel (p.114), open since 1905, is the pinnacle of luxury in Grand Canyon. If you've got the cash, there's no better place to stay. It's right on the rim, and several rooms offer canyon views. **Rates:** $340

★ BRIGHT ANGEL LODGE & CABINS

Also perched on the rim, this rustic lodge (p.136) has a bit of a split personality. Basic rooms (no private bath, showers down the hall) offer some of the best budget lodging in the park. Premium rooms and private cabins feature canyon views and working fireplaces. **Rates:** $100–$175

★ PHANTOM RANCH

Located at the bottom of Grand Canyon near the Colorado River, Phantom Ranch offers the only overnight lodging below the rim. Spending the night in the depths of Grand Canyon is one of the park's top experiences. See page 179 for more details. **Rates:** $61-$170

KACHINA & THUNDERBIRD LODGES

These blocky, utilitarian buildings, set about 60 feet back from the rim, are located between Bright Angel Lodge and El Tovar. The central location is a big plus, but there's not much in the way of rustic charm. Both lodges offer standard motel-style rooms with two queen beds. **Rates:** $311

MASWIK LODGE

Set a quarter-mile back from the rim, Maswik Lodge offers basic motel-style rooms. The lodge is divided into north and south sections (rooms in the north section are more spacious and offer more amenities). In summer, rustic cabins with two beds are available. **Rates:** $245

YAVAPAI LODGE

This is the largest lodge in the park. It's less popular than other lodges because it's situated half a mile from the rim, but it's also the most likely to have rooms on short notice. The lodge offers standard motel-style rooms at Yavapai East (with air conditioning) and Yavapai West (with ceiling fans). **Rates:** $202

For comprehensive lodging info visit jameskaiser.com

Camping

MATHER CAMPGROUND

Set in a lovely ponderosa forest near Grand Canyon Village, this campground has over 300 campsites. Each campsite accommodates up to six people, three tents, and two vehicles. (No RV hook-ups, 30-foot max. vehicle length.) Coin-operated hot showers and laundry are available nearby. Open year-round. Cost: $18 per night. Reservations, which are highly recommended April–October, can be made up to six months in advance (recreation.gov, 800-444-6777).

TRAILER VILLAGE

Located next to Mather Campground, this popular RV campground offers hook-ups for vehicles up to 50 feet in length. Open year-round. Cost: $52 per night. Reservations highly recommended April–October. Call 888-297-2757 for advance reservations, 928-638-2631 for same-day reservations.

DESERT VIEW CAMPGROUND

Located 26 miles east of Grand Canyon Village at Desert View (p.166), this campground is open mid-April through mid-October. The 50 campsites are first-come, first-served. Each campsite accommodates up to six people, three tents, and two vehicles. No showers, laundry, or RV hook-ups. Cost: $12 per night.

Inner Canyon Camping

There are two popular campgrounds in Grand Canyon, but they are only accessible on foot or by mule. Both campgrounds offer restrooms and running water. Reservations are issued as permits by the Backcountry Office (p.15).

INDIAN GARDEN CAMPGROUND

Located 4.6 miles down the popular Bright Angel Trail, Indian Garden Campground sits above the banks of Garden Creek, which is surrounded by shady cottonwood trees.

BRIGHT ANGEL CAMPGROUND

Located at the bottom of Grand Canyon between the Colorado River and Phantom Ranch, this beautiful campground is accessible from the South Rim via the Bright Angel Trail or South Kaibab Trail. There are 32 campsites above Bright Angel Creek. Each campsite has a picnic table and fire ring. If you don't want to lug camping gear, you can arrange for mules to carry up to 30 pounds of gear. Call 888-297-2757 for more information about mule "Duffel Service."

For comprehensive camping info visit jameskaiser.com

Dining

Most South Rim restaurants are located in Grand Canyon Village. During peak season, restaurants that don't accept reservations fill up fast, and wait times can sometimes exceed two hours. If you want to beat the crowds, arrive before the post-sunset rush.

★ EL TOVAR DINING ROOM $$$ (Brk, Lnch, Din)

For over 100 years, El Tovar Dining Room has offered the finest dining on the South Rim. This is Grand Canyon's priciest restaurant, but the soft lighting, dark wood paneling, and rustic luxury are worth it. Reservations (required for dinner) are available up to six months in advance (928-638-2631 x6432).

★ ARIZONA ROOM $$$ (Lnch, Din)

The South Rim's second-best restaurant, located next to Bright Angel Lodge, serves steakhouse favorites and Southwestern fare. The pleasant atmosphere includes large picture windows with canyon views. No reservations. Arrive early to beat the crowds.

BRIGHT ANGEL RESTAURANT $$$ (Brk, Lnch, Din)

The South Rim's third-best restaurant offers steakhouse favorites, Southwestern specialties, and some salad and veggie options. No reservations.

CANYON VILLAGE DELI $$$ (Brk, Lnch)

Your best bet for inexpensive take-out sandwiches, plus salads and baked goods. Located in the Canyon Village Market.

MASWIK PIZZA PUB $$$ (Lnch, Din)

Fresh-baked pizza, wings, draft beer, and sports on TV. Located in Maswik Lodge adjacent to the cafeteria.

MASWIK CAFETERIA $$$ (Brk, Lnch, Din)

Cafeteria-style food. Located in Maswik Lodge.

YAVAPAI CAFETERIA $$$ (Brk, Lnch, Din)

Cafeteria-style food. Located in Yavapai Lodge.

Cocktails

★ EL TOVAR LOUNGE (11am–11pm)

The best place to enjoy a drink on the South Rim. Relax in El Tovar's sumptuous surroundings or head to the outdoor patio and enjoy the canyon views. Draft beer, wine, creative cocktails, light appetizers.

Activities

RANGER PROGRAMS

Free ranger programs are one of the best ways to learn about Grand Canyon National Park. There are geology talks, fossil walks, California condor discussions, guided hikes, and evening programs at the Shrine of the Ages Auditorium. Check the park's website (nps.gov/grca) or inquire at visitor centers for seasonal times and locations.

BUS TOURS

Xanterra (888-297-2757, grandcanyonlodges.com) offers narrated South Rim bus tours. The Desert View Tour (4 hours, $70) heads east along Desert View Drive. The Hermits Rest Tour (2 hours, $40) travels west along Hermit Road. Sunrise and sunset tours (1.5–2 hours, $30) are another great option. There's also a package deal that offers two tours for $85. Kids under 16 ride free when accompanied by a paying adult.

MULE RIDES

Day and overnight mule rides (p.19) depart daily from the South Rim. The two-hour Canyon Vistas Mule Ride ($143), which heads east of Yaki Point along the East Rim Trail, departs at 9am and 1pm. Overnight mule rides follow the Bright Angel Trail to the bottom of Grand Canyon, where riders spend the night at Phantom Ranch (p.179), then return via the South Kaibab Trail ($693 for one person, $1,204 for two people). Rides offering two nights at Phantom Ranch are also available ($1,010 for one person, $1,658 for two people). Reservations, which should be made as early as possible, are accepted up to one year in advance (888-297-2757, grandcanyonlodges.com).

GRAND CANYON STAR PARTY

Grand Canyon boasts some of the darkest, clearest skies in the United States. Local astronomy clubs celebrate this fact each June with an eight-night Star Party. The free event features speakers from Arizona astronomy clubs and plenty of telescopes aimed at the stars. Dates vary depending on the new moon.

GRAND CANYON MUSIC FESTIVAL

This popular music festival features concerts in late August and early September at the Shrine of the Ages Auditorium (grandcanyonmusicfest.org).

ART EXHIBITS

Kolb Studio (p.139) features regularly changing art exhibits.

GRAND CANYON VILLAGE

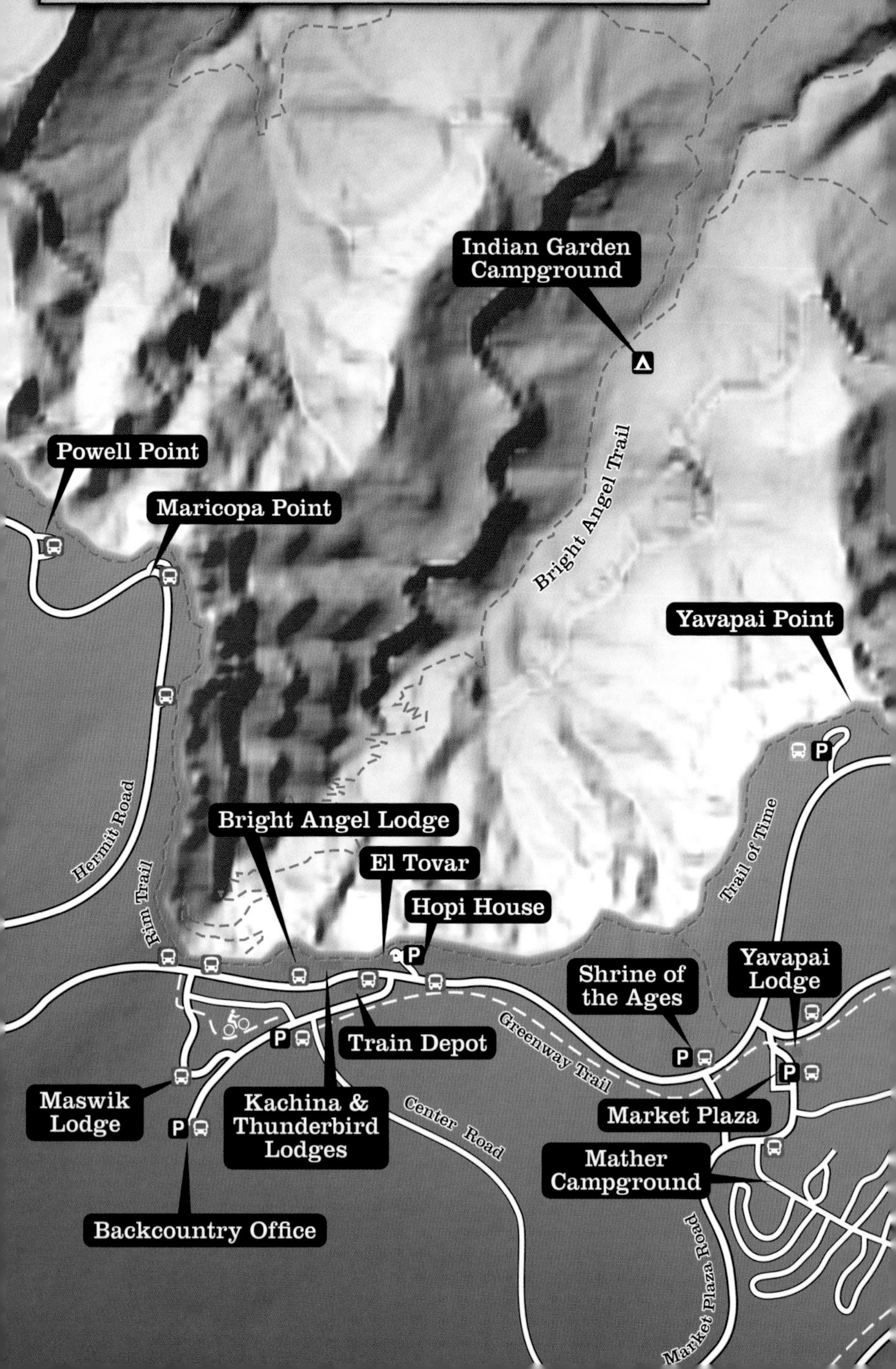

Indian Garden
Campground

Bright Angel Trail

Powell Point

Maricopa Point

Yavapai Point

Hermit Road

Rim Trail

Trail of Time

Bright Angel Lodge

El Tovar

Hopi House

Shrine of
the Ages

Yavapai
Lodge

Train Depot

Greenway Trail

Maswik
Lodge

Kachina &
Thunderbird
Lodges

Center Road

Market Plaza

Mather
Campground

Backcountry Office

Market Plaza Road

N

Tonto Trail

South Kaibab Trail

Mather Point

Grand Canyon
Visitor Center

Yaki Point

Trailer
Village

Yaki Point Road

uth Entrance Road

Desert View Drive

Pipe Creek Vista

Grand Canyon Visitor Center

This cluster of buildings is Grand Canyon's main visitor center, and it should be your first stop after entering the park. The main visitor center features a ranger-staffed information desk and interesting exhibits. Outside panels offer a wealth of additional information on everything from hiking to geology. A free 20-minute film, *Grand Canyon: A Journey of Wonder*, is shown every half-hour between 8:30am and 4:30pm. Directly across the way is the Visitor Center Park Store, a terrific shop operated by the non-profit Grand Canyon Conservancy that sells books, maps, and gifts. Next door, Bright Angel Bicycles rents bicycles and sells coffee, wraps, and sandwiches at its small café.

If you're only visiting the South Rim for the day, consider parking at the Visitor Center and exploring the South Rim via the park's free shuttle system. Parking is limited along the South Rim, and finding parking spaces can be hard, especially during peak season. Both the Village Route Shuttle (which services Grand Canyon Village) and the Kaibab Rim Route Shuttle (which services Yavapai Point, Yaki Point, and the South Kaibab Trailhead) make regular stops at the Grand Canyon Visitor Center.

Another great way to explore the South Rim without the hassle of driving is renting bicycles from Bright Angel Bicycles. The South Rim has roughly 13 miles of paved, automobile-free Greenway Trails perfect for biking, and the park's free shuttle buses have bicycle racks. See page 119 for more information on South Rim biking.

Mather Point

Mather Point is Grand Canyon's most popular viewpoint—but that's mostly due to its close proximity to the visitor center. The views *are* fabulous, however, and Mather Point's good eastern exposure makes it a wonderful place to watch sunrise.

As you stand at Mather Point, ponder the fact that just one-third of the total length of Grand Canyon is visible. At 277 miles, Grand Canyon is roughly *one-tenth* the length of the continental United States. But is it the largest canyon on earth? Technically, over a dozen other canyons are deeper or wider or longer. But no other canyon on earth is as deep *and* wide *and* long *and* geologically dramatic as Grand Canyon. (There is, however, an even more impressive canyon in our solar system: Valles Marineris on Mars, which is nine time longer, seven times deeper, and 37 times wider than Grand Canyon!)

Mather Point is named for Stephen Mather, a wealthy industrialist who became the first director of the National Park Service. In 1914 Mather complained to Interior Secretary Franklin Lane about the management of America's national parks. Lane's response: "If you don't like the way the national parks are being run, come on down to Washington and run them yourself." Mather did just that, spending the next 13 years shaping a strong vision for America's national parks.

Sunrise Tip!

If it's crowded at Mather Point, walk a few minutes east along the Rim Trail. You'll find plenty of great viewpoints with far fewer crowds.

Yavapai Point

This dramatic viewpoint offers the best views near Grand Canyon Village. Because Yavapai Point juts out relatively far into the canyon, you'll enjoy spectacular panoramas east and west—great for sunrise or sunset.

Yavapai Point's sweeping views made it the logical choice for Grand Canyon's first museum, which was constructed here in 1928. Today Yavapai Geology Museum remains one of the best places to learn about Grand Canyon geology. Inside you'll find fascinating exhibits on everything from the formation of rock layers to the carving of Grand Canyon by the Colorado River. Large picture windows make it a great place to take shelter on cold winter days or during summer thunderstorms. Park rangers often offer free afternoon geology talks.

One of Yavapai Point's most prominent sights is Bright Angel Canyon, which slices eight miles into the North Rim directly in front of the viewpoint. The North Kaibab Trail (p.276) runs through much of Bright Angel Canyon, connecting the North Rim to the Colorado River. Near the head of the canyon, look for a faint patch of green cottonwood trees. The trees mark the location of Phantom Ranch (p.179), which offers overnight lodging at the bottom of Grand Canyon.

Sunset Tip!

If it's crowded at Yavapai Point, head west along the Trail of Time to the beautiful, lesser-known viewpoints near the 140-million-year marker or off the spur trail that starts at the 440-million-year marker.

Trail of Time

This walking Grand Canyon timeline is a geologist's dream come true. Each meter represents one million years. So the 1.3-miles (2.1-km) trail, which stretches between Yavapai Geology Museum and Verkamp's Visitor Center, represents 2.1 *billion* years of Earth history. Nothing puts Grand Canyon's age in perspective like a stroll down the Trail of Time. The trail officially starts just west of Yavapai Geology Museum, but it's equally fascinating starting from Verkamp's. Bronze markers embedded in the path mark your location, and a series of exhibits discuss key aspects of Grand Canyon geology along the way. The opening/closing displays, which illustrate Grand Canyon rock layers, are constructed from actual rocks taken from the depths of the canyon.

Verkamp's Visitor Center

This historic building, located at the western end of the Trail of Time, has an information desk, bookstore, and exhibits about Grand Canyon's early pioneer history. The building was originally operated as "Verkamp's Curios" by John G. Verkamp, a Grand Canyon pioneer who began selling "curios" (unique gifts) to tourists in 1905. After Verkamp's death, his descendants carried on the family tradition until 2008, when the National Park Service acquired the building. The family's 103-year streak was the longest of any family-owned business in the national park system.

Hopi House

This rustic stone building celebrates the native cultures who call the Grand Canyon region home. Designed by architect Mary Colter (right), Hopi House's stone exterior, thatched ceilings, and mud-plastered interior walls are all characteristic of traditional Hopi architecture. Tiny windows let in a minimum of sunlight, keeping the interior cool and refreshing in summer. Colter even added romantic flourishes like corner fireplaces made from broken pottery. Although Colter incorporated many authentic Hopi details, she did forgo the traditional roof entrance in favor of a front door.

Hopi craftsmen performed much of the construction and masonry, and when Hopi House opened in 1905 native artisans lived on its upper floors. One family lived there for three generations. After working all day, artisans relaxed on the open-air terraces off the building's upper floors, enjoying beautiful views of Grand Canyon. The first floor of Hopi House was filled with native-made arts and crafts—Navajo rugs, Hopi Kachina dolls, baskets, pottery, jewelry—and every evening Hopi dancers performed outside. Hopi House offered Grand Canyon visitors an intriguing glimpse of the Southwest's indigenous cultures, just a few steps away from the luxurious El Tovar Hotel.

Today Hopi House continues its century-old tradition of selling authentic, high-quality native crafts. You can still find Navajo blankets and Hopi Kachina dolls for sale, as well as baskets, pottery, and jewelry from tribes across the Southwest. There's also a good selection of books about native culture.

Architect of the Southwest
MARY COLTER

Grand Canyon's most famous architect not only designed some of the most impressive buildings in the park—she did so in the early 1900s when almost no women practiced architecture. Breaking from tradition to imagine a new Southwestern aesthetic, Mary Colter created buildings that combined native culture, rustic romanticism, local materials, and deep respect for the region's beautiful landscapes.

As a young girl growing up in St. Paul, Minnesota, in the late 1800s, Mary Jane Colter was captivated by the artwork of local Sioux Indians. After graduating from the California School of Design in San Francisco, she was hired by the Fred Harvey Company to decorate the interior of an "Indian Building" at the Alvarado Hotel in Albuquerque, New Mexico. Fred Harvey operated a string of successful hotels and restaurants along the Santa Fe Railway, and he knew eastern travelers were fascinated by the indigenous people of the Southwest—and eager to buy their beautiful rugs and baskets. Colter threw herself into the project, designing a tasteful space that not only displayed native crafts for sale but paid homage to the cultures behind them. Recognizing Colter's talent, the Fred Harvey Company hired her to design a new Indian Arts Building next to the new luxury hotel it was planning at Grand Canyon: El Tovar.

The design of Hopi House, as the building came to be called, was a striking contrast to the luxurious El Tovar. Whereas El Tovar was inspired by European chalets, Hopi House was inspired by Old Oraibi, a 900-year-old pueblo 80 miles west of Grand Canyon. Instead of playing it safe with popular European styles, Colter embraced local native architecture. She immersed herself in the minutiae of Hopi design, meticulously studying construction details. When it was time to build Hopi House, she insisted on working with local materials that blended seamlessly with the natural environment. Her goal was to complement the landscape, not compete with it.

Hopi House opened to wide acclaim, and Mary Colter went on to design some of Grand Canyon's most famous buildings: Lookout Studio, Hermits Rest, Phantom Ranch, Bright Angel Lodge, and her masterpiece: Desert View Watchtower. A woman of strong will and boundless energy, Colter ruffled many feathers. She was a perfectionist who drove workmen crazy in her quest to create perfectly imperfect designs. Although Colter's buildings were often romanticized, they reflected a genuine desire to create something timeless. Today her buildings are among the most celebrated and popular in Grand Canyon.

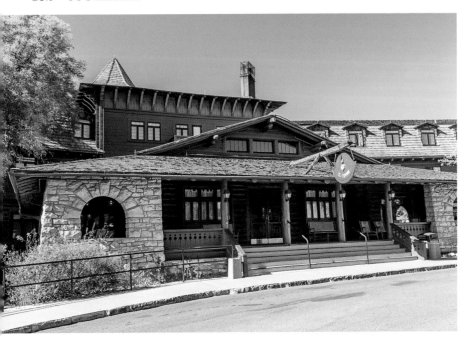

El Tovar Hotel

This historic hotel—the "Ritz of the Divine Abyss"—offers the finest lodging in Grand Canyon. Over the years, El Tovar has played host to such 20th-century luminaries as Theodore Roosevelt and Albert Einstein. Even if you're not a guest, El Tovar's dramatic front lobby is worth a quick look, and its bar and restaurant offer the best food and drinks on the South Rim.

When El Tovar opened in 1905, it was one of the most technologically advanced hotels in the Southwest. Among its high-tech amenities: electric lights, steam heat, indoor plumbing, and hot water—a stark contrast to the primitive rooms, cheap beds, and outhouses that previously defined luxury at Grand Canyon. Fresh fruits and vegetables were grown in El Tovar's greenhouses, and local farm animals provided fresh eggs and milk. El Tovar was the brainchild of the Atchison, Topeka, and Santa Fe Railway, which wanted a grand hotel to accommodate the flood of tourists arriving by train. Its architect, Charles Whittlesey, was inspired by Swiss chalets and Norwegian villas.

El Tovar was named after Don Pedro de Tovar, a lieutenant of Spanish explorer Francisco Vázquez de Coronado, who led the first Spanish expedition through the Southwest in 1540. Ironically, Don Pedro de Tovar never visited Grand Canyon. Coronado sent another of his men, García Lopez de Cárdenas, to explore Grand Canyon. When the Fred Harvey Company decided to build the hotel, however, they already had a Cárdenas Hotel in Colorado, so they went with the name El Tovar instead.

The Battleship

This long, prominent rock formation, named for its physical resemblance to a battleship, is home to a cave used by nesting California condors (p.60).

North Rim (p.247)

Bright Angel Canyon
Slicing eight miles into the North Rim, this dramatic side canyon is home to the North Kaibab Trail (p.276)

Plateau Point (p.111)

Indian Garden
Easily distinguished by its green canopy of cottonwood trees, this lush oasis was once used as a garden by native tribes. Today Indian Garden Campground is used by backpackers on the Bright Angel Trail.

Bright Angel Trail (p.170)

Bright Angel Lodge

Perched along a particularly dramatic section of the South Rim, Bright Angel Lodge is worth a quick glimpse inside. You'll find a small museum with historic photos and a fireplace built out of actual Grand Canyon rocks, arranged floor to ceiling in their proper geological sequence. A small booth to the left of the front desk offers information on ranger programs, bus tours, mule rides, and other South Rim activities.

The original Bright Angel Hotel offered the first overnight accommodations in Grand Canyon Village. When it opened in 1896, guests could stay at the hotel or in an adjacent tent camp. Guests walked from the tent camp to the hotel along an elevated boardwalk that protected them from mud and horse droppings (a prominent feature of Grand Canyon Village back then). Over the years, the lodge expanded to include a log cabin with eight guest rooms. Cabin rooms rented for $2.50 per night, and tents rented for $1.50. The current buildings were designed by architect Mary Colter in the 1930s.

Geological Fireplace

Santa Fe Train Depot

This rustic train station, located just south of El Tovar Hotel, is the only train station in a U.S. national park. It's also said to be the last active train station in America built entirely out of logs.

Train service arrived at the South Rim in 1901, following the completion of a spur line connecting the South Rim to the town of Williams (60 miles south). Before the spur line was completed, the most dependable form of transportation to the South Rim was a bumpy, all-day stagecoach ride that cost $20. When the spur line was completed, visitors could travel to the South Rim in four hours for $3.50. Not surprisingly, the railroad brought a steady stream of new visitors to Grand Canyon. Within a few decades, however, most people were arriving by car, and in 1968 falling ridership forced the railroad to shut down. The last departing train carried only three passengers. Then, in 1989, the railroad roared back to life. With traffic and congestion increasing in the park, a new generation of riders rediscovered the charm and convenience of the railroad. Today trains depart daily from Williams (p.116).

Lookout Studio

This small stone building, located on the edge of the canyon just west of Bright Angel Lodge, offers stunning views from its outdoor patio. Lookout Studio was designed by Mary Colter, who wanted the building to blend seamlessly into the landscape. This followed the design principles set forth by landscape architect Frederick Law Olmstead, who believed that, whenever possible, buildings in national parks should reflect the architecture of indigenous cultures. The indigenous cultures of the Southwest built some of the most impressive structures in America, and Colter incorporated many of their architectural techniques—stone walls, flat roofs, timber supports—into her design. After it was built, Lookout Studio became famous for its sweeping views. An old Santa Fe Railroad brochure boasted that visitors who peered through the telescopes installed at Lookout Studio could "traverse the Canyon trails, explore the rugged portions of the interior, or see its faraway reaches."

Lookout Studio, 1915

Kolb Studio

This building, perched precariously at the edge of the canyon, is currently home to an art gallery with changing exhibits. But for over 70 years, it was the home of Emery Kolb, one of Grand Canyon's earliest and most famous photographers. Emery and his brother Ellsworth came to Grand Canyon in 1902. They set up a photography studio on the rim and sold souvenir photos of mule riders descending the nearby Bright Angel Trail. As *Saturday Evening Post* writer Irvin S. Cobb wrote of one such mule ride, "Just under the first terrace a halt is made while the official photographer takes a picture; and when you get back he has your finished copy ready for you, so you can see for yourself just how pale and haggard and wall-eyed and how much like a typhoid patient you looked."

Tourist photos paid the bills, but the Kolbs' real passion was exploring Grand Canyon and capturing their daredevil exploits on film. In 1911 the brothers ran the Colorado River from Wyoming to California—the first successful attempt since John Wesley Powell in 1869. The brothers filmed their journey and made the first-ever movie of a Grand Canyon river trip. The Kolbs screened the movie at lectures across the country, and it played continuously at Kolb Studio until Emery's death in 1976.

Emery Kolb

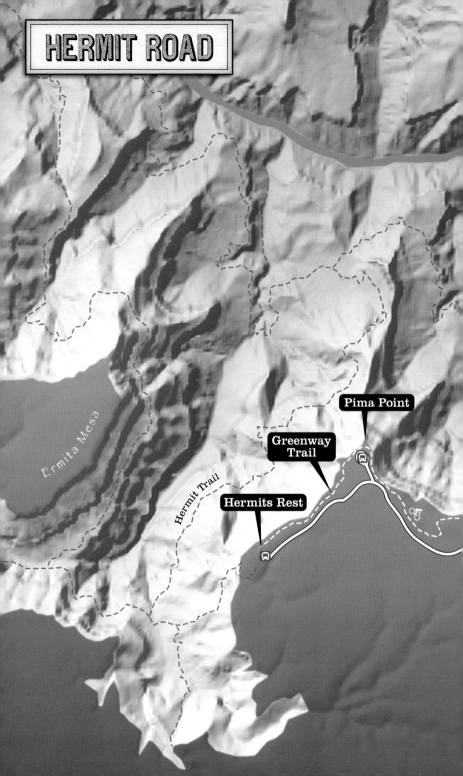

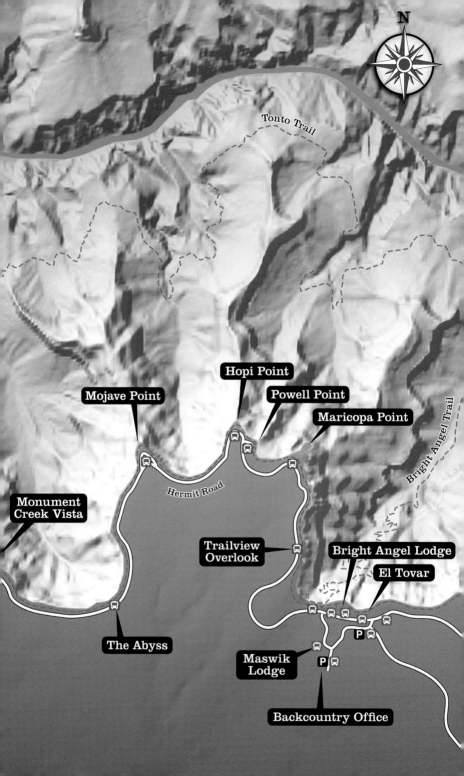

N

Tonto Trail

Hopi Point

Mojave Point

Powell Point

Maricopa Point

Bright Angel Trail

Hermit Road

Monument
Creek Vista

Trailview
Overlook

Bright Angel Lodge

El Tovar

The Abyss

Maswik
Lodge

P

P

Backcountry Office

Maricopa Point

Maricopa Point offers Hermit Road's first dramatic views of western Grand Canyon. Just west of the viewpoint are the remains of the Orphan Mine, one of America's most productive uranium mines in the 1950s. Prior to the 1950s, the mine site was home to a 20-cabin resort owned by Will Rogers, Jr.

Sentry Milk-vetch
(*Astragalus cremnophylax*)

Grand Canyon is the only place in the world where you can find this tiny, beautiful, endangered plant. Sentry milk-vetch grows in cracks in Kaibab Limestone (Grand Canyon's top rock layer) within 25 feet of the rim. Its scientific species name, *cremnophylax*, means "gorge watchman." Although just one inch tall and six inches in diameter, it boasts up to 200 lavender flowers each spring. Today just 2,500 sentry milk-vetch remain, and Maricopa Point is home to the largest population (roughly 600 plants). In 2008 a parking area was removed at Maricopa Point to create additional habitat for sentry milk-vetch. A fence now protects the delicate plants.

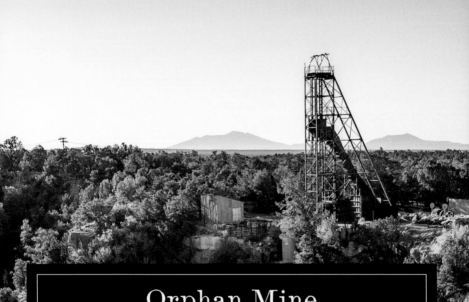

Orphan Mine

This former mine, located between Maricopa Point and Powell Point, was one of the country's most productive uranium mines in the 1950s and '60s. The Orphan Mine claim patent was originally filed in 1906 by Dan Hogan, and it was signed by his old commandant in the Spanish-American War: President Teddy Roosevelt. Copper and other metals were extracted from the Orphan Mine in the early 1900s, and in 1951 high-grade uranium was discovered roughly 1,500 feet below the surface. Although the land around the mine was federally protected from mining activities, the mine itself was considered a private inholding established prior to the creation of the national park. In 1956 a private company began uranium mining operations. Several years later, they discovered rich veins of ore that extended beyond the mine's original boundaries. The company strong-armed the government into expanding the mine's boundaries by threatening to build a 600-room, 18-story hotel on the site. In 1962 President John F. Kennedy signed a law that expanded mining operations near the Orphan Mine in exchange for the title to the claims within 25 years.

The Orphan Mine closed for good in 1969, by which point over 4.2 million pounds of uranium had been extracted. (It has been estimated that northern Arizona contains roughly 326 million pounds of uranium—the energy equivalent of 11.6 billion barrels of oil.) In 1987 the National Park Service obtained the title to the Orphan Mine, and today the Rim Trail detours around the mine due to concerns of lingering radiation.

Powell Point

Powell Point is named for John Wesley Powell (p.87), the famous explorer who led the first Colorado River expedition through Grand Canyon in 1869. In 1920 a monument to Powell was built and dedicated here. The ceremony was attended by Powell's niece and grand-niece, and the monument was christened by the secretary of the interior with water from the Colorado River. (Ironically, Powell Point has no views of the Colorado River.)

Powell's Grand Canyon adventure has been called the last great expedition of the American West. Prior to the trip, no one knew what existed along much of the Colorado River. There were rumors of giant waterfalls at the bottom of Grand Canyon and places where the river disappeared underground. Accepting these risks, Powell, a one-armed Civil War veteran, and nine other men, none with any whitewater experience, launched four boats from Green River, Wyoming, in May 1869. Three months later, two boats carrying six skeletal men emerged from Grand Canyon near present-day Lake Mead. Four men had abandoned the grueling journey along the way, three of whom died trying to reach civilization. The names of those four men do not appear on the monument.

Zoroaster Temple

Hopi Point

Hopi Point is the northernmost point on Hermit Road. Jutting far out into the canyon, it offers sweeping views that stretch from Vishnu Temple (p.159) in the east to Havasupai Point in the west. If you're traveling west on Hermit Road, Hopi Point also provides your first glimpse of the Colorado River. For all of these reasons, Hopi Point is one of Grand Canyon's most popular viewpoints, attracting dozens, sometimes *hundreds* of people for sunrise and sunset.

As you enjoy the views, notice the impressive stone "temples" rising from the depths of the canyon. These pointy rock formations reminded geologist Clarence Dutton (p.38) of ancient Asian and Middle Eastern temples when he surveyed

Vishnu Temple

Grand Canyon in the 1870s. Dutton was tasked with naming prominent rock formations, and he chose names from eastern religions to reflect the awe they inspired. Zoroaster Temple, Osiris Temple, Isis Temple, and Vishnu Temple are just a few of the dramatic formations visible from Hopi Point.

Sunrise/Sunset Tips!

There's only one downside to Hopi Point sunsets: big crowds. If you don't mind waking up early, catch the pre-dawn shuttle to enjoy sunrise, which attracts far fewer people. If your heart's set on sunset, hike west from Hopi Point on the Rim Trail to escape the commotion. Or, even better, take the shuttle to Mohave Point or Pima Point, which offer similar views with fewer crowds.

Mohave Point

Not only can you see the Colorado River from Mohave Point, you can see three of its famous rapids: Hermit Rapid (above), Granite Rapid, and Salt Creek Rapid. There are over 160 rapids in Grand Canyon, ranging in difficulty from 1 to ten. (Grand Canyon uses its own rating system for rapids where ten roughly translates to Class V on other rivers). Although rapids account for just ten percent of the Colorado River's 277 miles in Grand Canyon, they account for nearly half of its 2,000-foot elevation drop. Rapids often form next to side canyons, where flash floods (p.17) dump rocks and debris into the Colorado River. This constricts the river, backing it up and creating a steep drop-off, which forms the rapid. A few rapids in Grand Canyon drop up to 30 feet in a matter of seconds, creating some of the most thrilling whitewater in North America.

Mohave Point is named in honor of the Mojave Indians, who once lived along the lower Colorado River south of Grand Canyon. (As a general rule, "Mojave" is spelled with a "j" in California and with an "h" in Arizona.)

Sunset Tip!

Most sunset worshippers head to Hopi Point, which is famous for sweeping east-west views. Although Mohave Point's eastern views are partially blocked by Hopi Point, Mohave Point has equally dramatic western views, making it a terrific—and less crowded—choice for sunset. If crowds are still an issue, walk west along the Rim Trail to more secluded spots—including a few with picnic tables.

The Abyss

This appropriately named viewpoint showcases one of Hermit Road's most dramatic sections. From the canyon's edge, sheer cliffs plunge nearly 3,000 feet. The next shuttle stop to the west, Monument Creek Vista, also offers impressive views of the terrifying drop-offs. Both viewpoints offer a terrific glimpse of Grand Canyon's top six rock layers (p.33), which represent 80 million years of earth history.

Pima Point

Pima Point offers one of the best views of the Colorado River along Hermit Road. It's named after the Pima Indians of southern Arizona, who call themselves *Akimel O'odham* ("River People"). The name "Pima" is derived from *pim'ach* ("I don't understand you"), which was probably what the *Akimel O'odham* said when early Spanish explorers asked them what they called themselves.

In 1912 the Fred Harvey Company built a cluster of tent cabins called Hermit Camp 3,600 feet below Pima Point. Hermit Camp was located along the Hermit Trail, the Santa Fe Railroad's free alternative to the Bright Angel Trail, which was then privately owned. Hermit Camp boasted showers, telephones, a dining hall, a stable, and a blacksmith's shop. Guests stayed for several days, spending their time exploring the rugged surroundings on foot or horseback.

In 1926 the Fred Harvey Company built a 6,300-foot aerial tram connecting Pima Point and Hermit Camp. At the time it was the longest single-span tram in America, and the ride was about 30 minutes each way. In the late 1920s, however, the park gained control of the Bright Angel Trail and lifted its $1 per person toll. Before long, most visitors were descending the canyon via the Bright Angel Trail, which is closer to the park's hotels. In 1930 Hermit Camp shut down.

Hermits Rest

Hermits Rest marks the end of Hermit Road. Its main attraction is a whimsical stone building with a giant fireplace. Drinks, snacks, and gifts are available inside. Restrooms are located nearby. Hermits Rest was built by the Santa Fe Railroad in 1914. Like many famous buildings in the park, it was designed by architect Mary Colter, who wanted to create a building that looked like the kind of place a hermit might live. In addition to the main building, she also designed a limestone arch with an authentic mission bell from New Mexico.

The "hermit" of Hermits Rest was an early prospector named Louis Boucher, who lived by himself in the canyon below. Although labeled a hermit, Boucher was, by all accounts, a friendly man who simply liked living alone. Originally from Quebec, Boucher arrived at Grand Canyon around 1891. Like many prospectors, he had several horses and mules. Unlike many prospectors, he kept goldfish in a small trough. Boucher planted an orchard that provided him with peaches, oranges, and figs. But after spending two decades searching in vain for a rich mineral strike, Boucher packed his bags, left Grand Canyon, and moved to Utah.

Louis Boucher

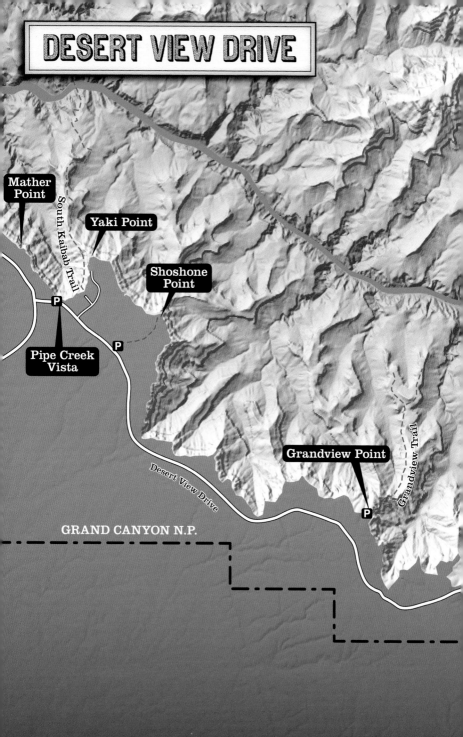

DESERT VIEW DRIVE

Mather Point

South Kaibab Trail

Yaki Point

Shoshone Point

P

P

Pipe Creek Vista

Grandview Point

Grandview Trail

Desert View Drive

P

GRAND CANYON N.P.

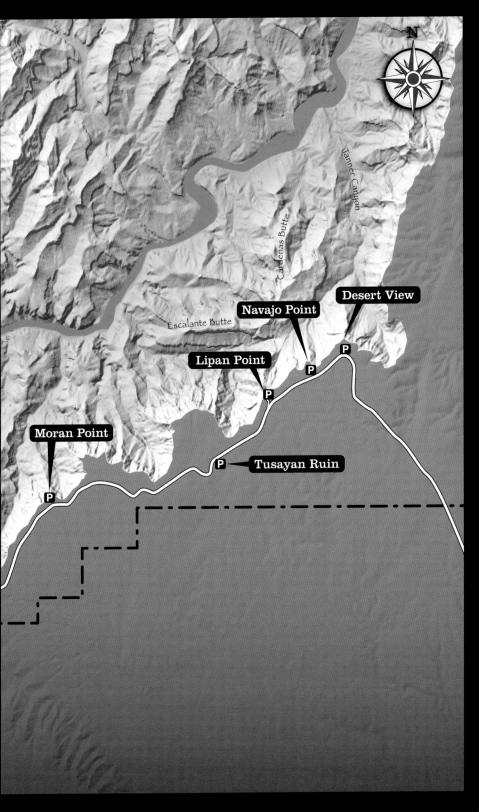

Yaki Point

Located at the tip of a prominent finger of land, Yaki Point (elevation 7,262 feet) provides sweeping views east and west. This is one of the best sunrise/sunset spots on the South Rim. And because the road to Yaki Point is closed to private vehicles, it's generally less crowded than other, more accessible viewpoints. The easiest way to get to Yaki Point is via the free shuttle that departs from Grand Canyon Visitor Center. There's also an early morning Hikers' Express shuttle (see Sunrise Tip below). Another option is walking or biking to the South Kaibab Trailhead, then following Yaki Point Road to the viewpoint.

As you stare into the canyon, notice O'Neil Butte (above). Try to spot the faint line carved into its eastern flank. That's the South Kaibab Trail (p.180)—the most direct route to the bottom of Grand Canyon. Unlike most inner canyon trails, which are tucked into deep side canyons, the South Kaibab Trail descends along an open ridge with spectacular views. To see for yourself, hike partway down the trail, which starts near Yaki Point. Ooh-ah Point and Cedar Ridge are two of the most popular day hiking destinations. During peak season you can also join a free ranger-led hike partway down the South Kaibab Trial (check park publications for seasonal schedules).

Sunrise Tip!

If you're spending the night at a hotel in Grand Canyon Village, the pre-dawn Hikers' Express shuttle, which stops at Bright Angel Lodge and the Backcountry Information Center, offers the fastest, most direct route to Yaki Point.

Shoshone Point

This gorgeous viewpoint boasts some of the South Rim's most incredible scenery. But getting to Shoshone Point requires a one-mile stroll along an unmarked trail, so relatively few people visit. The "hike" (elevation change: 50 feet) to Shoshone Point follows a dirt access road 1.3 miles east of the Yaki Point turnoff (6.3 miles west of Grandview Point). The trail starts at a locked metal gate that's easy to walk around. Don't worry, hiking here is 100% OK unless Shoshone Point has been reserved for a wedding or other private event. After a roughly 20-minute walk, you'll come to a picnic area with tables, grills, and pit toilets. Shoshone Point is located at the end of the prominent rock ledge nearby.

"The eye is at once caught by an object which seems to surpass in beauty anything we have yet seen. It is a gigantic butte, so admirably designed and so exquisitely decorated that the sight of it must call forth an expression of wonder and delight ... We named it Vishnu's Temple. "

-Clarence Dutton, 1882

Vishnu Temple

Rising to a maximum height of 7,533 feet, the pyramidal spire of Vishnu Temple is easily recognizable from many viewpoints along Desert View Drive. Like many prominent landmarks in Grand Canyon, Vishnu Temple was named by the geologist Clarence Dutton (p.38). Vishnu Temple is named for Vishnu, the four-armed Supreme Being of Hinduism. Hardcore rock climbers scramble to the top of Vishnu Temple, but it's considered one of the most difficult climbs in Grand Canyon. It was first climbed in 1946 by father-son team Merrel and Roger Clubb when Roger was just 19.

Grandview Point

At 7,400 feet, Grandview Point is one of the highest viewpoints on the South Rim. It's also the jumping-off point for the popular Grandview Trail (p.190). The trail dates from the early 1890s, when prospectors built it to haul copper ore out of the Grandview Mine (aka the Last Chance Mine), located on Horseshoe Mesa below. The mine contained an extremely high-grade ore—up to 70 percent copper—and in 1893 miners hauled out a 700-pound copper nugget. But when copper prices crashed in 1907 the mine shut down. In 1971 a mineralogist conducting research at Grandview Mine discovered a beautiful turquoise mineral (below), which was later classified as a brand new mineral species: Grandviewite.

Before the railroad arrived at Grand Canyon Village in 1901, Grandview Point was the South Rim's main tourist hub. In 1886 John Hance (p.89) built Grand Canyon's first hotel here, and a few years later a prospector named Pete Berry built the Grandview Hotel nearby. When the railroad arrived, however,  few tourists were willing to make the rugged journey to Grandview Point, and by 1908 both hotels shut down. A few years later, Berry sold his landholdings to newspaper tycoon William Randolph Hearst, who tore down Grandview Hotel in 1929. Hearst wanted to build a luxury hotel at Grandview Point, but a federal court forced him to sell his land to the park in 1939.

Moran Point

This impressive overlook is named after Thomas Moran, one of America's most famous and influential landscape painters. Born in England in 1837, Moran moved to America with his family in the mid-1800s. At the time landscape painting exhibitions drew blockbuster crowds in Eastern cities. In the days before color photography, monumental landscape paintings offered the public a rare glimpse of America's wild and exotic places. Inspired by these works, young Thomas Moran decided to become a landscape painter, and his dramatic paintings of Yellowstone were critical to the establishment of Yellowstone National Park in 1872. The following year, Moran joined legendary explorer John Wesley Powell on an expedition to Grand Canyon. He later wrote of his experience, "it was by far the most awfully grand and impressive scene that I have ever yet seen." Moran later returned with geologist Clarence Dutton, and his works from both of these trips were published in best-selling books. One of his paintings, *The Grand Chasm of the Colorado*, hung in the U.S. Capitol for many years. Deeply moved by his Grand Canyon experiences, Moran returned to the canyon every winter for over two decades.

Tusayan Ruin & Museum

These partially exposed ruins are the most impressive and accessible archaeological site on Grand Canyon's South Rim. Crumbling stone walls are all that remain of the small village that existed here roughly 800 years ago—three centuries before European contact. An easy, 0.1-mile path circles the ruins, and the adjacent museum has interesting displays exploring Grand Canyon's rich native history, from Ancestral Puebloans to modern tribes. Free ranger-led tours of Tusayan Ruin are sometimes offered (inquire at the museum).

At its peak, Tusayan Pueblo was probably home to no more than 20 or 30 Ancestral Puebloans. Archaeologists believe the site was occupied for just 25 years between A.D. 1185 and A.D. 1210. In fact, Tusayan was one of the last Ancestral Puebloan sites occupied in Grand Canyon. It was constructed just before the mysterious collapse of this once-dominant culture, which thrived across the Southwest for over 1,000 years (p.74).

Tusayan's most prominent structure was a 14-room building with storage rooms and living quarters. The single-story structure was built with stone, adobe, and wood. Living quarters stretched roughly east-west, and two storage areas branched off at right angles to form a central plaza. Many, if not most, daily activities took place in the outdoor plaza. Because it faced south, the plaza enjoyed abundant sunshine in the cold winter months.

Both living quarters and storage rooms lacked doors, which helped keep out animals. Villagers entered the rooms via wooden ladders poking out of small openings in the roof. Storage rooms contained stacked corn cobs, dried meats, and clay pots filled with dried beans and pinyon pine nuts. This surplus food, gathered in times of abundance, helped Ancestral Puebloans survive the lean winter months.

Adjacent to the main plaza were two round, ceremonial structures called kivas. These sacred buildings played an important role in the spiritual lives of Ancestral Puebloans. Villagers entered the kiva through a small opening in the roof, called the *sipapu*, then descended a wooden ladder into a dark chamber lit by fire. Kivas are representations of the *sipapuni*, where humans emerged from the underworld. Modern descendents of Ancestral Puebloans, including the Hopi, believe the sipapuni is located in the depths of Grand Canyon (p.74). Although kivas were often built underground, the hard Kaibab Limestone at Tusayan favored above-ground structures.

The residents of Tusayan hunted mule deer and jackrabbits, gathered wild plants, and grew beans, corn, and squash. Because there is no permanent water source within seven miles of Tusayan, villagers built stone walls to gather runoff during summer thunderstorms. Additional water was stored in clay pots and woven baskets that were water-proofed with pinyon pine pitch.

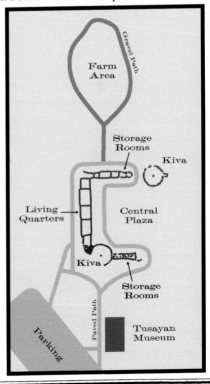

There is much that remains unknown about Tusayan Pueblo, but perhaps the greatest mystery is why the Ancestral Puebloans decided to build a village at a location with no natural water source. The answer may be more spiritual than practical. The main plaza offers impressive views of the distant San Francisco Peaks, which are considered sacred by regional tribes. And just north of Tusayan lies Grand Canyon, where humans are said to have emerged. Situated between two points of great spiritual significance, Tusayan may have been an appeal to the gods by a culture facing decline.

Lipan Point

This dramatic viewpoint is the best place to see rocks from the Grand Canyon Supergroup, which are absent from much of Grand Canyon. To spot the rocks, look north towards a sharp bend in the Colorado River. Directly above the river bend you'll notice colorful rock layers tilted at a distinct 20-degree angle. This is the Grand Canyon Supergroup, which ranges in age from 800 million to 1.2 billion years old, making them among the oldest rocks in Grand Canyon. Take a moment to ponder their age. When they formed plants and land animals had not yet evolved, and Earth's continents were barren rocks, more similar to Mars than the landscapes we know today.

Just below the Grand Canyon Supergroup, the Colorado River twists around broad, circular Unkar Delta. Roughly 1,000 years ago, Unkar Delta was home to a farming community of Ancestral Puebloans (p.74). Archaeologists believe as many as ten families may have lived there. The farmers built stone houses and planted corn, beans, and squash on terraces along Unkar Creek, which flows through the delta. In summer, when the bottom of Grand Canyon became uncomfortably hot, the families hiked to the North Rim to tend farms on its broad, flat plateaus. After harvesting North Rim crops, they returned to Unkar Delta. For generations they repeated this annual cycle. Then, for reasons not fully understood, the ancient farmers abandoned their homes. Today Unkar Delta contains the largest complex of archaeological sites along the Colorado River in Grand Canyon.

Navajo Point

Rising 7,461 feet above sea level, Navajo Point is the highest viewpoint on the South Rim. Its sweeping panorama is nearly as dramatic as nearby Desert View—with a fraction of the crowds. To the east Desert View Watchtower rises like a tiny speck against the horizon. To the north the Colorado River emerges from the narrow walls of Marble Canyon, then curves west into the sprawling heart of Grand Canyon, twisting through an enormous maze of mesas and buttes.

Navajo Point is named after the Navajo Tribe (p.75), whose 17-million-acre reservation reaches its western limit along the east rim of Grand Canyon. Navajo legend speaks of a Visionary who, standing on the rim of Grand Canyon, witnessed a secret Nightway Ceremony conducted by the gods in the depths of the canyon. When the gods saw Visionary, they decided he must learn the Nightway Ceremony, so he was sent to sacred sites throughout Navajo territory. Visionary's final journey was floating through Grand Canyon on a log with his pet turkey. Upon emerging from the canyon, Visionary was taken to a cave where all the gods gathered to give him final instructions. Harvest God then transported Visionary to Canyon de Chelly, where he taught his family the Nightway Ceremony. Even today, it remains an important Navajo ritual.

Desert View Watchtower

This circular tower is considered architect Mary Colter's (p.131) masterpiece in Grand Canyon. Inspired by the stone towers built hundreds of years earlier by Ancestral Puebloans (p.74), Desert View Watchtower serves as a cultural gateway to the region's native tribes.

Colter spent six months researching and planning the tower, which was constructed in 1932. "First and most important," she wrote, "was to design a building that would become a part of its surroundings—one that would create no discordant note against the time-eroded walls of this promontory." The frame is made of steel, but stone, plaster, and wood give it a rustic, weathered look. At 70 feet tall it dwarfs any archaeological tower in the Southwest. But Colter wasn't interested in a replica. She was interested in stunning views from a tall building that blended into the landscape—a problem that seemed "unsolvable" until she realized native architects developed a solution hundreds of years earlier.

Visitors enter Desert View Watchtower through the Kiva Room. In Puebloan culture, kivas are ceremonial chambers used for religious and political gatherings. In actual kivas, smoke from the central fire pit purifies those ascending the ladder above. From the Kiva Room a series of narrow stairways lead to circular viewing platforms. Paintings by Hopi artist Fred Kabotie depict gods and legends on the first platform. Upper levels contain replicas of native Southwestern art by Fred Geary. Continue to the top floor, where large picture windows reveal the tower's most impressive feature: breathtaking, 360-degree views.

Native Art at Desert View

Desert View Watchtower is filled with paintings that pay homage to the region's native cultures. The Hopi Room, on the first floor, showcases paintings by Hopi artist Fred Kabotie (pictured here). The upper floors, painted by Fred Geary, are filled with reproductions of petroglyphs and pictographs from across the Southwest.

Sun   Moon   Thundercloud

The Snake Legend

This large circular painting depicts the Snake Legend, which tells the story of the first person to navigate the Colorado River in Grand Canyon. The story begins in the upper left, with a Chief giving Hopi prayer sticks to his son. The upper right depicts the son floating in a hollowed-out log down the Colorado River. Grand Canyon's steep walls rise on either side, and a thundercloud looms above. The lower right shows the son's meeting with the Snake Priest after his river trip. The Snake Priest gives the young man a bow, the symbol of the Snake Clan, and his daughter's hand in marriage. The final panel depicts the couple's honeymoon. Because the Snake Clan blessed the marriage, the bow drips rain and six different kinds of rain clouds form above. The four colors used in the backgrounds and outer rings represent the four cardinal directions. The circle in the center represents the heart of the universe.

Hopi Wedding

A Hopi bride heads to her wedding with hair decorated in squash blossom whorls. She carries piki bread, while two maidens follow her with corn meal. Shooting stars above scatter sacred corn meal from their tails.

Muyingwa

The god of germination holds a corn-stalk in his right hand. His left hand holds a planting stick, a bag of seeds, and a gourd filled with water. A thundercloud hovers above Muyingwa's head.

Stars

Multiple stars and constellations are depicted on the ceiling, including the Morning Star *Talashu* (above left), Evening Star *Mihekshuho* (above right), the Milky Way, the Pleiades (*Chochookam*), Corona borealis (*Lalakontu*), and the Big Dipper, which points to the North Star (*Queninkshu*).

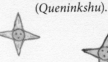

Hayapao

This large, winged figure represents the power and forces of the air. Above Hayapao's head is a rain cloud and a four-color rainbow that ends in two clouds.

⊰ BRIGHT ANGEL TRAIL ⊱

SUMMARY The Bright Angel Trail is Grand Canyon's most popular inner canyon hike. Although steep and challenging, it's well maintained and easy to follow. Because it starts near Grand Canyon Village, however, its upper reaches are consistently crowded. (Tip: the South Kaibab Trail and Hermit Trail offer similar hikes with fewer crowds.) The most popular day hikes are 1.5-Mile Resthouse (2–4 hours, round-trip) or 3-Mile Resthouse (4–6 hours, round-trip), both of which offer seasonally available water. Halfway down the trail is Indian Garden Campground, where a spur trail heads 1.5 miles to Plateau Point (p.175). Past Indian Garden, the Bright Angel Trail continues its descent, dropping 200 feet at Devils Corkscrew, a series of dramatic switchbacks through craggy Vishnu Schist. The trail ultimately connects with the River Trail and Bright Angel Suspension Bridge, which crosses the Colorado River en route to Bright Angel Campground and Phantom Ranch.

TRAILHEAD The Bright Angel Trail starts next to Kolb Studio, just west of Bright Angel Lodge.

◆ **TRAIL INFO** ◆

RATING: Strenuous

HIKING TIME: 2–3 days

DISTANCE: 15.6 miles, round-trip

ELEVATION CHANGE: 4,285 feet

BRIGHT ANGEL TRAIL

N

2,546 feet
Phantom Ranch

Bright Angel
Campground
2,480 feet

River
Resthouse
2,480 feet

1.8 miles   River Trail

Plateau
Point

1.5 miles

3.2 miles

Devils
Corkscrew

Tonto Trail

Tonto Trail

Indian Garden
Campground
3,800 feet

1.5 miles

Maricopa
Point

Yavapai
Point

3-Mile Resthouse
4,748 feet

Grand Canyon
Visitor Center

Mather
Point

1.5 miles

1.5-Mile Resthouse
5,729 feet

Hermit Road

1.5 miles

El Tovar

6,860 feet

Yavapai Road

Greenway Trail

Mather
Campground

South Entrance Road

Desert View Drive

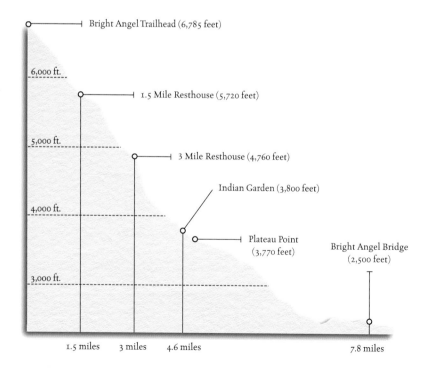

Bright Angel Trailhead (6,785 feet)

6,000 ft.

1.5 Mile Resthouse (5,720 feet)

5,000 ft.

3 Mile Resthouse (4,760 feet)

Indian Garden (3,800 feet)

4,000 ft.

Plateau Point
(3,770 feet)

Bright Angel Bridge
(2,500 feet)

3,000 ft.

1.5 miles   3 miles   4.6 miles   7.8 miles

BRIGHT ANGEL TRAIL

Plateau Point

Plateau Point is one of the inner canyon's most stunning destinations. Perched 1,300 feet above the Colorado River, it treats hikers and mule riders to 360-degree views of some of Grand Canyon's most famous landmarks. If you're spending the night in Indian Garden Campground on the Bright Angel Trail, Plateau Point makes a fantastic sunrise or sunset hike. The 1.5-mile trail to Plateau Point is reached via the Tonto Trail near Indian Garden Campground. After crossing Garden Creek just below Indian Garden, follow the Tonto Trail west for roughly three-quarters of a mile until reaching a fork. Turn right at the fork and walk across the broad, flat platform to Plateau Point.

Devils Corkscrew, Bright Angel Trail

Phantom Ranch

Nestled in a narrow canyon not far from the Colorado River, Phantom Ranch offers Grand Canyon's only overnight lodging below the rim. Eleven rustic cabins and two dormitories are scattered along the banks of Bright Angel Creek. Towering cottonwood trees provide welcome afternoon shade. A central dining hall serves home-cooked meals and sells cold beer. Showers and flush toilets add a touch of backcountry luxury. An overnight stay at Phantom Ranch is, without question, one of the highlights of Grand Canyon National Park. There are two common ways to spend the night here. Overnight mule rides ($693–$1,010 per person) start at the South Rim, with one or two nights of lodging at Phantom Ranch. Reservations for hikers ($61 dorm room, $170 private cabin) are granted via an online lottery, which opens 15 months in advance. Visit grandcanyonlodges.com for more info.

⊸ SOUTH KAIBAB TRAIL ᕟ

SUMMARY Steep and strenuous, the South Kaibab Trail is the most direct route to the bottom of Grand Canyon. While most inner canyon trails follow deep side canyons, the South Kaibab Trail follows open ridgelines, providing spectacular views in all directions. Day hikers can visit the aptly named Ooh Aah Point (1.8 miles, 1–2 hours round-trip) or Cedar Ridge (3 miles, 2–4 hours round-trip). Advanced hikers can head past O'Neil Butte to Skeleton Point (6 miles, 6–9 hours round-trip). The South Kaibab Trail ends at the Kaibab Suspension Bridge, which crosses the Colorado River. If you're planning to spend the night at Bright Angel Campground or Phantom Ranch, consider hiking down the South Kaibab Trail and returning via the Bright Angel Trail, which is longer but less steep. Note: there is no water on the South Kaibab Trail, and the trail's lack of shade can be dangerous in summer.

TRAILHEAD The trail starts near Yaki Point. Shuttles to the trailhead depart from Grand Canyon Visitor Center. An early morning Hikers' Express Shuttle also departs from Bright Angel Lodge and the Backcountry Information Center.

TRAIL INFO

RATING: Strenuous	**HIKING TIME:** 2 days
DISTANCE: 6.4 miles, one-way	**ELEVATION CHANGE:** 4,700 feet

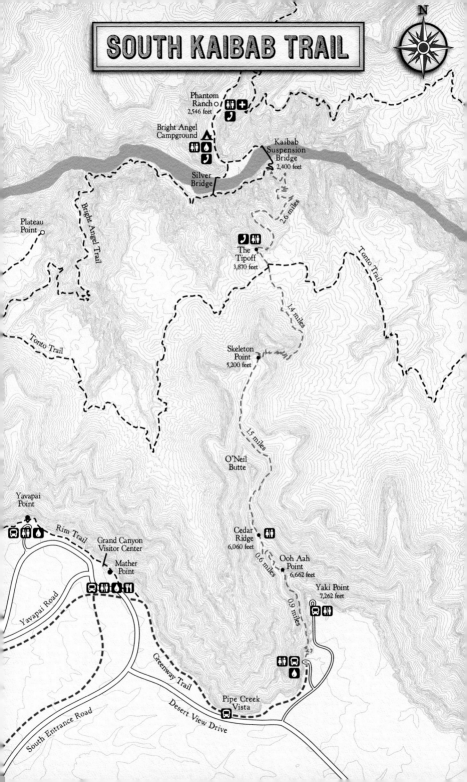

SOUTH KAIBAB TRAIL

N

Phantom Ranch
2,546 feet

Bright Angel
Campground

Kaibab
Suspension
Bridge
2,400 feet

Silver
Bridge

Plateau
Point

Bright Angel Trail

2.6 miles

The Tipoff
3,870 feet

Tonto Trail

Tonto Trail

1.4 miles

Skeleton
Point
5,200 feet

1.5 miles

O'Neil
Butte

Yavapai
Point

Rim Trail

Grand Canyon
Visitor Center

Mather
Point

Cedar
Ridge
6,060 feet

0.6 miles

Ooh Aah
Point
6,662 feet

Yaki Point
7,262 feet

0.9 miles

Yavapai Road

Greenway Trail

Pipe Creek
Vista

South Entrance Road

Desert View Drive

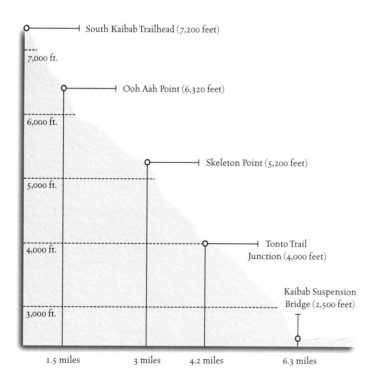

South Kaibab Trailhead (7,200 feet)

7,000 ft.

Ooh Aah Point (6,320 feet)

6,000 ft.

Skeleton Point (5,200 feet)

5,000 ft.

Tonto Trail
Junction (4,000 feet)

4,000 ft.

Kaibab Suspension
Bridge (2,500 feet)

3,000 ft.

1.5 miles   3 miles   4.2 miles   6.3 miles

South Kaibab Trail

❧ HERMIT TRAIL ❧

SUMMARY Although less famous than the popular Bright Angel Trail, the Hermit Trail is one of the South Rim's best hikes. Departing from Hermits Rest, it treats hikers to spectacular western vistas as it descends to the Colorado River in two steep drops. Though unmaintained, the Hermit Trail is generally in good condition, with a few tricky but manageable washouts. Day hikers can head 2.5 miles to Santa Maria Spring (5–8 hours, round-trip). The Hermit Trail ends along the banks of the Colorado River next to Hermit Rapid—one of the most thrilling rapids in Grand Canyon. If you're lucky, you'll catch a glimpse of river runners hooting and hollering as they barrel through the waves. Backpackers must camp at designated campsites at either Hermit Creek Campsite (located just west of the Hermit Trail along the Tonto Trail) or at Hermit Rapid.

TRAILHEAD The Hermit Trail starts west of Hermits Rest (p.152) at the end of Hermit Road. Overnight hikers can park at the trailhead (you'll be given a code to open the gate to Hermit Road). Day hikers can ride the free shuttle to Hermits Rest.

TRAIL INFO

RATING: Strenuous

HIKING TIME: 2–3 days

DISTANCE: 18.6 miles, round-trip

ELEVATION CHANGE: 4,240 feet

HERMIT TRAIL

N

Whites Butte

Travertine Canyon

Hermit
Rapid
2,300 feet

1.5 miles

Tonto Trail

2.7 miles

Cathedral
Stairs

Yuma
Point

Hermit Creek
Campsite
2,900 feet

Breezy
Point
4,420 feet

Eremita Mesa

Hermit Gorge

3.5 miles

Pima
Point

Boucher Trail

Hermit Road

6,640 feet
Hermits
Rest

Santa
Maria
Spring
5,000 feet

Dripping Springs Trail

2.2 miles

Waldron Trail

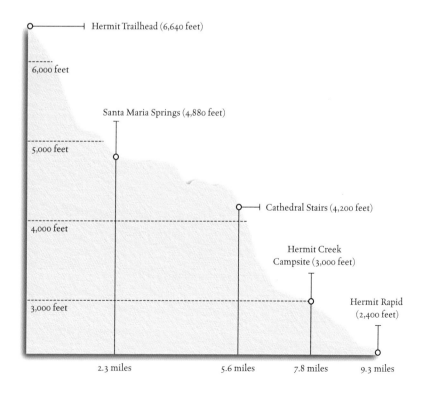

Hermit Trailhead (6,640 feet)

6,000 feet

Santa Maria Springs (4,880 feet)

5,000 feet

Cathedral Stairs (4,200 feet)

4,000 feet

Hermit Creek
Campsite (3,000 feet)

3,000 feet

Hermit Rapid
(2,400 feet)

2.3 miles   5.6 miles   7.8 miles   9.3 miles

HERMIT TRAIL

~ GRANDVIEW TRAIL ~

SUMMARY The steep Grandview Trail, which drops roughly 2,500 feet from Grandview Point to Grandview Mesa, is one of the few inner canyon trails that doesn't descend all the way to the Colorado River. Mellow day hikers can enjoy outstanding views along the first quarter-mile of the trail. Energetic day hikers can head all the way to the campground at Horseshoe Mesa (6–9 hours, round-trip). There are no water sources on Horseshoe Mesa, so backpackers must bring their own water for drinking and cooking. Several trails descend roughly 1,000 feet from Horseshoe Mesa to the Tonto Trail. If you're spending the night, a brief hike to the stunning overlook at the eastern tip of Horseshoe Mesa makes a great day trip. Note: there are many abandoned copper mines in the vicinity of Horseshoe Mesa. Do not enter abandoned mines, which can be extremely danger-ous due to steep drop-offs and toxic gases.

TRAILHEAD The Grandview Trail starts at Grandview Point (p.160), about 12 miles east of Grand Canyon Village on Desert View Drive. There is a parking area next to the trailhead.

▶ TRAIL INFO ◀

RATING: Strenuous	**HIKING TIME:** 1–2 days
DISTANCE: 6 miles, round-trip	**ELEVATION CHANGE:** 2,500 feet

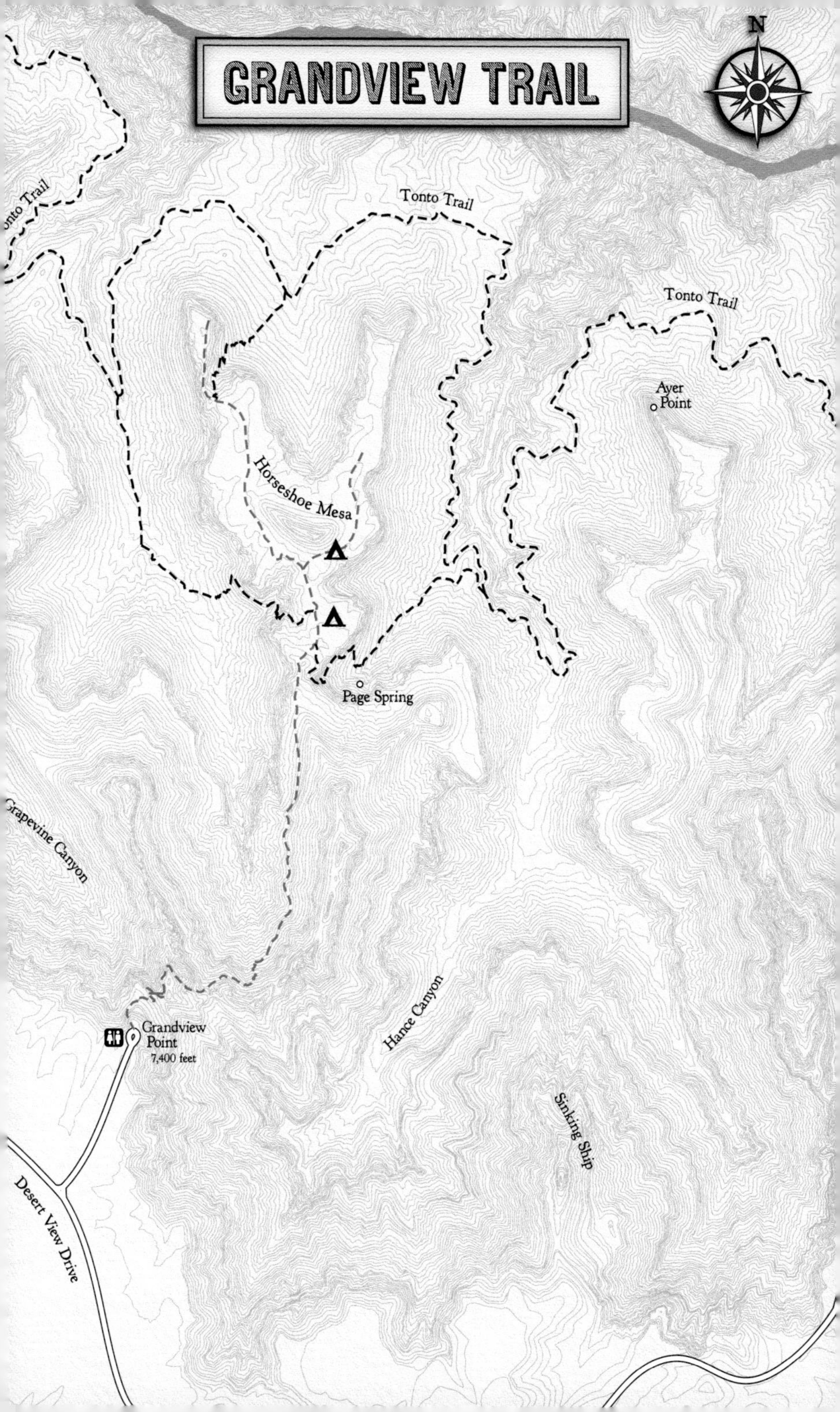
GRANDVIEW TRAIL
N
Tonto Trail
Tonto Trail
Tonto Trail
Ayer Point
Horseshoe Mesa
Page Spring
Grapevine Canyon
Grandview Point
7,400 feet
Hance Canyon
Sinking Ship
Desert View Drive

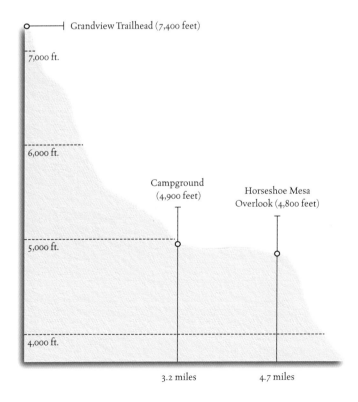

Grandview Trailhead (7,400 feet)

7,000 ft.

6,000 ft.

Campground
(4,900 feet)

Horseshoe Mesa
Overlook (4,800 feet)

5,000 ft.

4,000 ft.

3.2 miles

4.7 miles

GRANDVIEW TRAIL

COLORADO RIVER

THE COLORADO RIVER is the heart and soul of Grand Canyon. Without it, Grand Canyon would be just another flat stretch of land in northern Arizona. Instead, the river has cut a mile into the surrounding landscape, exposed nearly two billion years of earth history, and flushed out over 1,000 cubic miles of eroded debris. The result is the most impressive natural feature in North America.

As stunning as the view is from the rim, the view from the river is even more spectacular. Flowing downstream from Lees Ferry (just south of the Utah/Arizona border), the Colorado River enters the most scenic stretch of whitewater in America. As the river cascades down a series of thrilling rapids, sheer cliffs rise up thousands of feet on either side. Twisting deep into the heart of Grand Canyon, the river exposes a dazzling natural world filled with towering rock formations, sandy beaches, dark caverns, and sparkling waterfalls. Side canyons spread out in all directions, channelling unlikely streams through parched terrain. As the Colorado River flows around sharp bends, cool canyon shadows mingle with shimmering river light.

As the largest river in the Southwest, the Colorado is a river of liquid gold. Its water, delivered via massive aqueducts, allows millions of people to live in the desert and enables farmers to grow billions of dollars of crops year-round. Although plugged by dams and reservoirs along much of its length, the Colorado flows free in Grand Canyon for 277 miles, thrilling river runners who enjoy some of the most spectacular scenery in America.

Each year roughly 25,000 people—less than half of one percent of all park visitors—embark on a river trip through Grand Canyon. That number is strictly limited by the National Park Service to preserve the wilderness experience at the bottom of the canyon. Those lucky enough to witness Grand Canyon from the Colorado River are filled with awe. Physically, the size of Grand Canyon is humbling. Visually, it's one of the most dynamic places in the world, changing with the weather, the seasons, and the time of day. Even seasoned world travelers confess that a river trip through Grand Canyon is one of earth's most remarkable outdoor adventures.

NATURAL HISTORY

FROM START TO finish, the Colorado River passes through some of the most beautiful and varied terrain in North America. Born in the deep gorges of the upper Rocky Mountains, it plunges headfirst down pine-covered slopes to emerge in the desert Southwest. The river cuts through the wind-swept canyons of Utah, tears deep into Grand Canyon, and glides through the California desert. By the time it crosses the Mexican border en route to the Sea of Cortez, the river has passed through seven Western states and drained an area the size of Iraq.

The Colorado River is often referred to as the "Nile of America." At first glance, this comparison seems appropriate. Both rivers pass through vast deserts and both sustain millions of people along the way. But despite these similarities, the rivers share little else in common. In terms of size, the Colorado is much smaller, draining just a quarter of the land the Nile drains. In terms of length, the 1,400-mile Colorado pales in comparison to the 4,000-mile Nile.

Even in America, the Colorado lacks many impressive statistics. It's not the longest river in America. Six other rivers are longer. Nor is it the biggest river in America. In terms of annual flow, the Colorado doesn't even rank in the top 25. But what the Colorado does have, and what makes it so remarkable, is the wildest and most terrifying elevation drop of any major river in North America.

From its headwaters in the Rocky Mountains to the Gulf of California, the Colorado plummets over 13,000 vertical feet. This steep drop, occurring over a relatively short distance, churns up a river that's fast and furious, dropping an average of 7.7 feet per mile—25 times steeper than the mighty Mississippi. Because a river's erosive power increases exponentially with its speed, the Colorado would be a highly destructive river in any part of the world. But in the desert Southwest—a crumbling landscape filled with soft rocks and sparse vegetation—its erosive power is monumental.

As the Colorado enters the desert Southwest, it grinds away at the region's barren rocks, picking up tiny particles of sediment along the way. The more sediment the river picks up, the more abrasive it becomes. The more abrasive it becomes, the more sediment it picks up. This vicious cycle feeds on itself until the Colorado is, quite literally, a river of liquid sandpaper. Before massive dams plugged the Colorado, the river's sediment loads were phenomenal. Back then, the Colorado carried an average of 235,000 tons of sediment through the Grand Canyon *each day*. "Too thick to drink, too thin to plow," was how one early explorer described it. The river's composition was often two parts sediment to one part water, and because the sediment had a high concentration of iron oxide the virgin Colorado had a distinct reddish hue.

The virgin Colorado was also psychotically unpredictable. Early explorers often compared it to a bull. It was an "angry bull," a "blooded bull," and a "wild bull of destruction." The Colorado's flows in Grand Canyon varied anywhere

COLORADO RIVER BASIN

N

IDAHO

NEVADA

WYOMING

Flaming
Gorge Reservoir

COLORADO

Great
Salt Lake

UPPER COLORADO

Salt
Lake
City

RIVER BASIN

Green River

Gunnison River

Colorado River

UTAH

Lake
Powell

San Juan River

NEW MEXICO

Las
Vegas

Lake
Mead

Little Colorado River

IFORNIA

LOWER COLORADO

Albuquerque

RIVER BASIN

Salt River

Phoenix

Gila River

ARIZONA

Sea of Cortez

between 3,000 and 200,000 cubic feet of water (90 to 6,000 tons) per second, sometimes within a matter of weeks. The largest flows occurred in spring, when snowmelt from the Rocky Mountains set loose months of accumulated precipitation. In any given year, snowmelt accounts for over 70 percent of the Colorado River's flow.

The Colorado's spring floods were biblical in proportion. Roaring through the Southwest, they ripped out vegetation, eroded huge chunks of the riverbank, and tumbled 20-ton boulders like ice cubes. During these floods, the river carried its heaviest sediment loads, devouring the landscape at an astonishing rate.

By winter, however, the Colorado slowed to a trickle and hovered just above freezing—a stark contrast to summertime highs when the river often topped 80 degrees. An entire ecosystem evolved to live in these harrowing conditions. The humpback chub, a fish found only in the Colorado, has a life cycle timed to the

SEDIMENT LOAD

The amount of sediment a river can carry increases to the sixth power of its speed. A river flowing at 2 mph carries 64 times more sediment (2^6=64) than a river flowing at 1 mph (1^6=1). Likewise, a river flowing at ten mph carries one million times more sediment than a river flowing at 1 mph. During spring floods, the virgin Colorado often flowed at speeds topping 40 mph, carrying up to 27 million tons of sediment through Grand Canyon *each day*. During these floods, Grand Canyon experienced its most intense erosion.

river's wild temperature swings. It also has strong muscles and an uncanny sense of fluid dynamics to keep from washing away during spring floods. Plants were also influenced by flooding. Apache plume, mesquite, and catclaw acacia grew only above the flood zone.

As the Colorado River travels to the Sea of Cortez, it passes through an amazing diversity of landscapes. In Grand Canyon alone, the river encounters three of North America's four deserts. Vegetation typical of the Great Basin Desert, found in Nevada and western Utah, is visible from Lees Ferry to river mile 39. At river mile 39, the Colorado enters the northernmost reaches of the Sonoran Desert, which covers much of Arizona, Southern California, and northern Mexico. At river mile 157, the Colorado enters the Mojave Desert, the smallest of North America's four deserts but home to such national treasures as Death Valley and Joshua Tree National Park.

The Colorado River in Grand Canyon is on average 300 feet wide and 25 feet deep. Within Grand Canyon, the river is essentially a series of long pools interrupted by short, quick rapids. Although rapids account for only ten percent of the Colorado's 277-mile length in Grand Canyon, they account for nearly half of its 2,000-foot elevation drop. And the velocity of water in rapids is up to ten times greater than the long pools in between. On most rivers, rapids form wherever the riverbed drops naturally, but in Grand Canyon rapids form next to side canyons where flash floods dump debris into the Colorado. The debris constricts the river and backs it up, creating a steep drop-off that forms the rapid. Some of these rapids, which drop up to 30 feet in a matter of seconds, are considered among the most thrilling whitewater in North America.

CERTAIN DEATH

In 1849 an American Indian who spoke no English attempted to describe the Colorado River to would-be river runner William Manly. Using a stick to draw in the sand, he mapped the upper Colorado passing through mountains, valleys, and canyons. He then piled up stones to represent the deepest canyon of all. According to Manly, the Indian "stood with one foot on each side of his river and put his hands on the stones and then raised them as high as he could, making a continued e-e-e-e-e-e as long as his breath would last, pointed to the canoe and made signs with his hands how it would roll and pitch in the rapids and finally capsize and throw us all out. He then made signs of death to show us that it was a fatal place. I understood perfectly from this that below the valley where we now were was a terrible [canyon], much higher than any we had passed, and the rapids were not navigable with safety."

THE NEW COLORADO

TODAY GRAND CANYON is an oasis of uninterrupted whitewater on a river plugged with dams. Below Grand Canyon, Hoover Dam holds back Lake Mead, the largest man-made lake in the Western Hemisphere. Above Grand Canyon, Glen Canyon Dam holds back Lake Powell, the second-largest man-made lake in the Western Hemisphere. Almost all of the water that enters Grand Canyon now passes through the turbines at Glen Canyon Dam, which has significantly altered the downstream ecology.

Since Glan Canyon Dam's floodgates closed in 1963, the Colorado River in Grand Canyon has undergone a dramatic transformation. Its flow, temperature, and sediment load—the defining characteristics of the river—have completely changed. Other than the path it follows, the new Colorado bears almost no resemblance to the pre-dam river.

Historically, the amount of water flowing through Grand Canyon was determined by the amount of precipitation that fell on the Colorado River Basin. Today, the amount of water flowing through Grand Canyon is determined by the engineers at Glen Canyon Dam. Maximum flows are capped at less than ten percent of what they once were, and the massive spring floods that created much of Grand Canyon have been eliminated. This lack of flooding has created several problems. Most notably, much of the debris that washed into the river through side canyons now lies dormant on the bottom of the river. Before the dam, spring floods cleared out the debris and washed it downstream.

Although Glen Canyon Dam smoothed out the river's seasonal flows, daily flows became wildly erratic. The amount of water released from the dam is based on the region's fluctuating power demand, and during peak hours in the afternoon dam operators can charge twice as much for electricity as they can at night. When Glen Canyon Dam first opened, daily flows fluctuated anywhere between 3,000 and 31,500 cubic feet per second. Downstream, the river rose and fell like a toilet bowl. Daily tides often topped 13 feet and beaches along the banks of the river eroded at an unnaturally high rate. In 1992 Congress passed the Grand Canyon Protection Act, which required dam operators to smooth out releases in an attempt to reduce beach erosion.

Glen Canyon Dam also affected the Colorado River's sediment load. Ninety percent of the sediment that used to enter Grand Canyon is now trapped behind Glen Canyon Dam. Each year Lake Powell fills up with more and more sediment—a problem that future generations will have to contend with. In the meantime, water from Lake Powell enters Grand Canyon almost completely silt-free.

The water released by Glen Canyon Dam is drawn from the chilly depths of Lake Powell, entering Grand Canyon at a constant 45 degrees. Not surprisingly, this frigid water has significantly altered the Colorado's ecosystem. For millions of years, native fish had their life cycles timed to the Colorado's wild temperature

Disappearing Beaches

Before Glen Canyon Dam was constructed in 1963, the banks of the Colorado River in Grand Canyon were lined with hundreds of sandy beaches. Replenished each spring by the virgin Colorado's annual floods, the beaches provided valuable habitat for native species and were used as campsites by river runners. But following the construction of Glen Canyon Dam, the Colorado River's sediment load in Grand Canyon was reduced by 90 percent, and the beaches started to erode. Adding to the problem were the dam's erratic releases, which were timed to coincide with daily fluctuations in power demand. The dam releases created huge tides that stripped additional sand from the beaches and flushed it out of Grand Canyon.

In 1992 President George H.W. Bush signed the Grand Canyon Protection Act, which ordered Glen Canyon Dam to operate in a way that protected and enhanced Grand Canyon National Park, including smoothing out daily releases. Maximum flows were capped at 26,000 cubic feet per second (cfs), and daily fluctuations were limited to 8,000 cfs.

Scientists believed that smoothed-out flows would significantly reduce Grand Canyon beach erosion. But to their dismay, beach erosion continued at a steady rate. It turned out that new sediment deposited by tributary streams—

enough, theoretically, to replenish the beaches—was languishing at the bottom of the river. What Grand Canyon needed, the scientists concluded, was an old-fashioned flood to stir up the sediment and redeposit it on the riverbank.

In March 1996 Secretary of the Interior Bruce Babbitt turned the wheel at Glen Canyon Dam to release a controlled flood of 45,000 cfs. The flood churned up the river and created more than 50 new beaches. Within a year, however, many of those beaches had disappeared. The flood, it turned out, didn't so much create new beaches as wash existing beaches farther downstream. Some scientists blamed the failure on the timing of the flood. Most tributary streams deposit new sediment into Grand Canyon during the rainy summer season. But the flood was conducted in the spring, when much of the new sediment had already been washed out of the canyon. In 2004 a second controlled flood was released in November, when the river contained significantly more sediment. Since 1996 eight controlled floods have roared through Grand Canyon. The long-term effects of these floods are still being monitored.

In the end, the controlled floods stirred up as much controversy as they did sediment. And as the Southwest continues to grow, each drop of water in Lake Powell becomes ever more valuable. Many oppose sacrificing this water to test unproven theories, but something needs to be done before Grand Canyon's

swings. They could survive in cold winter water, but they also needed warm summer water to spawn. Now that warm water has disappeared, Grand Canyon's native fish have been forced to spawn in a handful of small tributaries.

As spawning grounds disappeared, so did the fish. Of Grand Canyon's eight native fish species, three have disappeared. Among those lost is the Colorado pikeminnow, which grows up to six feet long and can weigh over 100 pounds. The humpback chub, one of the few native species that remains, has been pushed to the brink of extinction. Scientists estimate that only a few thousand humpback chub remain in Grand Canyon. Adding to the problem are non-native sport fish that were introduced to the river. New arrivals such as trout, catfish, and carp, which thrive in the chilly water, compete with native fish for habitat and food.

Although the new Colorado wreaked havoc with native fish populations, it allowed other life forms to thrive. The cool, clear, sediment-free water allows sunlight to penetrate its depths, fostering the growth of algae. The abundance of algae forms the foundation of a healthy food chain. It has also turned the river a gorgeous shade of green.

Even the riverbank has undergone a major ecological change. For millions of years, the annual spring floods scoured the sides of the river. Now that flooding has been eliminated, a dense thicket of plants has taken up residence in the previous flood zone. This explosion of plants has led to dramatic increases in animal habitat and biodiversity.

In the end, the construction of Glen Canyon Dam radically changed the ecology of the Colorado River in Grand Canyon. Although many conservationists want the dam removed and the Colorado River returned to its natural state, Glen Canyon Dam is unlikely to be decommissioned anytime soon. It provides valuable water and electricity to a region starved for both. And although the river's ecology has been shaken up, there have been some improvements. The new river supports more plants and animals than the old one did, and its regulated flow allows hundreds of river runners to safely navigate Grand Canyon each year.

HUMAN HISTORY

ALTHOUGH THE COLORADO River is often hard to see from the rim of Grand Canyon, the canyon itself is visible from space. Equally impressive is the view from space at night, when the desert is filled with dense clusters of light that mark the booming cities of the Southwest. Over the past few decades, millions of people have flocked to cities like Phoenix, Tucson, and Las Vegas, eager to leave cold winters elsewhere behind. This phenomenal migration, which continues today, would have been impossible without water from the Colorado River. In a land of little rain, the Colorado is a river of liquid gold that has allowed the Southwest to flourish.

Today billions of dollars of agriculture, billions of dollars of industry, and millions of daily lives revolve around the Colorado River. Never before in human history have so many people and such an enormous economy been so dependent on a single source of water. It is, without question, the most important natural resource in the West. But the Colorado River is a limited resource, and huge demands have been placed on it. Today its flow is so regulated and its water so overused that not a single drop reaches the sea. And as the Southwest continues to grow, so do demands on the river. As a result, the Colorado has become one of the most argued over, litigated, politicized, and controversial rivers in the world.

The first attempt to tap the Colorado River was a disaster. In the late 1800s, a developer named Charles Rockwood realized that, given a steady source of water, the California desert could be turned into an agricultural paradise. If the Colorado River could be tapped and controlled, California farmers could grow crops year-round.

In 1901 a diversion channel was cut into the Colorado River. Overnight, California's previously bone-dry Imperial Valley became one of the most productive agricultural regions on the planet. But because the Colorado ran thick with sediment, the diversion channel silted up and the Colorado jumped its banks, tearing off in a totally new direction. Instead of draining into the Gulf of California, the Colorado flowed into the middle of Southern California. For the next three years, the river dumped its entire flow into the desert lowland area known as the Salton Sink. By the time engineers were able to redirect the river, an inland sea roughly one-third the size of Rhode Island had formed. The Salton Sea still exists there today.

The Colorado River was a force to be reckoned with, but there was too much money at stake to give up trying to tame it. The arid West was on the verge of a massive economic expansion, and savvy politicians realized its future was linked directly to the Colorado River. In the end, there was only one solution: build a massive dam that could regulate the Colorado, hold back its floods, and store them in a reservoir for later use.

In 1933 construction began on Hoover Dam. It was the biggest dam the world had ever seen. It tamed the Colorado, generated enormous amounts of electricity, and allowed the desert to bloom. Hoover Dam was such a resounding success that the government agency responsible for its creation, the Bureau of Reclamation, quickly became the golden child of American politics. Using the momentum generated by Hoover Dam, the bureau set off on a dam-building boom that lasted for the next 30 years.

The construction of so many expensive dams created economic windfalls in the states where they were built. Across the country, dam building was a politically charged process, but on the Colorado River the issue was even more complex. In 1922 a document called the Colorado River Compact had been drafted to allocate water from the Colorado River to the seven Colorado River Basin states. The compact divided the region into an Upper Basin and a Lower Basin, each receiving 7.5 million acre-feet of water per year. It was up to the states to figure out how to divvy up the water after that.

Not surprisingly, the Colorado River Compact set off vicious water wars between the states. Water was essential to each state's growth, and there wasn't enough to go around. The only way for a state to secure long-term water rights was to put that water to use before another state did. The result was the hasty construction of massive multi-billion dollar irrigation projects that made little practical sense. In a few short decades, 19 dams had been built on the Colorado River and its tributaries, and the river had been sucked dry.

Despite these problems, the Bureau of Reclamation continued to push for giant new dams. In 1963 Glen Canyon Dam was constructed to the furor of conservationists. When two more dams were proposed within Grand Canyon, the conservationists went wild. Led by David Brower of the Sierra Club, they used congressional hearings, letter writing campaigns, and modern media savvy to defeat the dams (p.73).

The bureau's defeat in Grand Canyon signaled a dramatic shift in popular opinion. Throughout much of the 20th century, dams had been viewed as glorious symbols of progress. But as the environmental movement took hold, many people began viewing dams as hulking symbols of man's interference with nature. Before long, the era of massive dam building was brought to a close.

The media blitz that defeated the dams also focused tremendous attention on the Colorado River in Grand Canyon. Soon, many ordinary people wanted to see it for themselves. Prior to 1950, fewer than 100 people had paddled the Colorado River through Grand Canyon. By 1970, roughly 15,000 people were making the trip each year. To reduce crowding, the park service began limiting the number of river runners. Today roughly 25,000 people run the Colorado through Grand Canyon each year. And while the river as a whole is submerged in controversy, the uninterrupted stretch of whitewater in Grand Canyon remains one of the most rugged and beautiful places in the world.

THE COLORADO RIVER COMPACT

In 1922 delegates from seven Western states gathered outside Santa Fe, New Mexico, to allocate water from the Colorado River. Their negotiations resulted in the Colorado River Compact, which was hailed as a "Constitution for the West." In reality, it was one of the most poorly conceived agreements in American history.

The Colorado River Compact "solved" the issue of water ownership by splitting the Colorado River Basin into two: an Upper Basin (Utah, Wyoming, Colorado, New Mexico) and a Lower Basin (California, Arizona, Nevada). Of the estimated 17 million acre-feet of water flowing through the Colorado River each year, each basin would receive 7.5 million acre feet. Mexico would receive the remaining two million acre feet. The Colorado River Compact left it up to the states to divvy up the water after that. Not surprisingly, the agreement touched off vicious water wars. Tensions flared and relationships frayed, but the worst was yet to come.

In 1953 the government admitted there was a fatal flaw in the Colorado River Compact. The original document, written during a period of unusually high rainfall, overestimated the river's annual flow by roughly 3 million acre-feet. States that fought tooth and nail over every last drop of the Colorado River were now faced with the gut-wrenching fact that there was almost 20 percent less water than originally thought. The water wars grew even more heated, and they remain so to the present day.

THE COLORADO RIVER
in
GRAND CANYON

Kanab Canyon

Matkatamiba Canyon

Lava Falls

Whitmore Wash

Shivwits Plateau

Havasu Can

National Canyon

*Hualapai
Indian
Reservation*

Diamond Creek

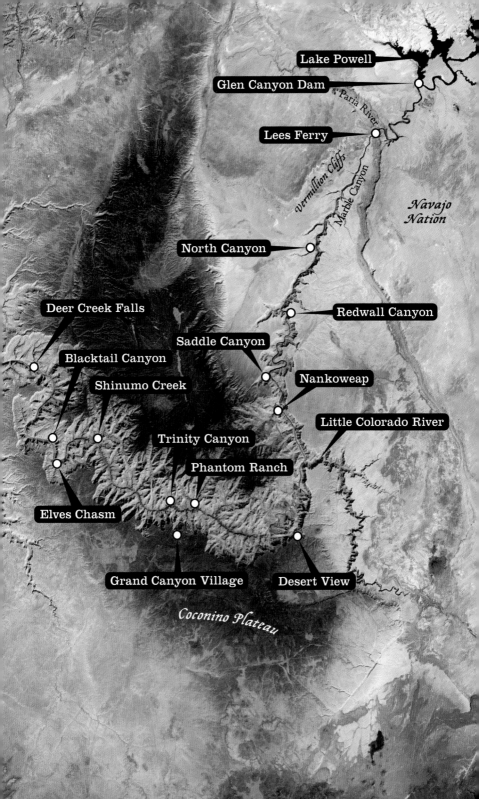

Glen Canyon Dam

This massive dam, located 15 river miles north of Grand Canyon, holds back Lake Powell, the largest man-made reservoir in the Western Hemisphere (capable of holding over eight trillion gallons of water). Glen Canyon Dam is 710 feet tall and 300 feet thick at the base, and it contains over 4.9 million cubic yards of cement. It took seven years to build and cost $272 million in 1963 dollars. If the dam's eight generators operated at full capacity, the dam could release 15 million gallons of water a minute and generate roughly 1.3 million kilowatts of electricity.

Since Glen Canyon Dam went into operation in 1963, it has completely altered the downstream ecology of the Colorado River in Grand Canyon. Many conservationists loathe Glen Canyon Dam. In addition to the ecological changes it has wrought, the dam flooded Glen Canyon—by many accounts one of the most beautiful places in the Southwest. Supporters of the dam claim Lake Powell is equally beautiful, and they point out that Glen Canyon Dam provides a steady source of clean, carbon-free energy.

But the attitudes of some former supporters have started to change. In 1997 former Arizona Senator Barry Goldwater, who originally supported the dam, came out against it in a PBS miniseries based on the book *Cadillac Desert*. "I have to be honest with you," he said, "I'd be happier if we didn't have the lake." Goldwater went on to say that, given the chance, "I'd vote against it. I've become convinced that, while water is important, particularly for those of us who live in the desert, it's not that important."

Lees Ferry (river mile 0)

Lees Ferry is the first place north of Grand Canyon where motor vehicles can access the Colorado River. As a result, it's the launching point for most Grand Canyon river trips. The next vehicle-accessible stretch of the Colorado River is Diamond Creek, 225 miles downstream.

In 1776 Spanish missionary Silvestre Vélez de Escalante visited this spot and declared: "It has an agreeably confused appearance." It was also the only viable river crossing for hundreds of miles. For nearly a century it was known as Paria Crossing after the nearby Paria River, which deposits five times more sediment into the Colorado than all other Grand Canyon tributaries combined. (Some of the Paria River's sediment comes from dissolved hoodoos in Bryce Canyon.)

Paria Crossing became Lees Ferry in 1872 after Mormon renegade John D. Lee established a ferry service there. A few years earlier, Lee participated in the Mountain Meadows Massacre, where Mormon vigilantes slaughtered 120 pioneers traveling to California. In 1870 the Mormon church excommunicated Lee, who fled to Grand Canyon. A few years later he was captured, tried, and executed by firing squad. The ferry operated until 1928, when it capsized and killed three people. The following year, Navajo Bridge opened five miles downstream.

Lees Ferry is the official boundary between the Upper and Lower Colorado River Basins. Across from the boat launch, a concrete pillar monitors the amount of water flowing from one basin to the next. The lives of 40 million people who depend on Colorado River water are directly affected by that pillar.

View from Navajo Bridge

Marble Canyon (river miles 0–61)

Marble Canyon gives river runners their first taste of the power and beauty of Grand Canyon. Its steep, narrow walls offer dramatic scenery broken up by dozens of exciting rapids. But there's no marble in Marble Canyon. The name was given by John Wesley Powell, who thought the sedimentary rocks, polished smooth by muddy river water, resembled marble.

In the 1960s, the U.S. Bureau of Reclamation wanted to build a dam at river mile 39. Had the dam been built, the upper reaches of Marble Canyon would have been flooded. Public pressure ultimately defeated the bureau's plan.

> "We have cut through the sandstones and limestones met in the upper part of the canyon, and through one great bed of marble a thousand feet in thickness. In this, great numbers of caves are hollowed out, and carvings are seen which suggest architectural forms, though on a scale so grand that architectural terms belittle them. As this great bed forms a distinctive feature of the canyon, we call it Marble Canyon."
>
> —John Wesley Powell

Vasey's Paradise

This beautiful spring gushes from a cave in the Redwall Limestone. As John Wesley Powell noted, "We find fountains bursting from the rock high overhead, and the spray in the sunshine forms the gems which bedeck the wall. The rocks below the fountain are covered with mosses and ferns and many beautiful flowering plants. We name it Vasey's Paradise, in honor of the botanist who traveled with us last year." Grand Canyon's Redwall Limestone is riddled with caves and aquifers, including one that feeds Vasey's Paradise. The lush vegetation here supports eight species of mollusks, including the endangered, inch-long Kanab ambersnail.

"The water sweeps rapidly in this elbow of river, and has cut its way under the rock, excavating a vast half-circular chamber, which, if utilized for a theater, would give seating to 50,000 people. Objection might be raised against it, however, for at high water the floor is covered with a raging flood."

—John Wesley Powell

Redwall Cavern

North Canyon

Saddle Canyon

Nankoweap (river mile 53)

Nankoweap is one of Marble Canyon's most beautiful destinations. In addition to spectacular scenery, this graceful bend in the river is home to famous archaeological sites, great camping, and terrific hiking.

The origin of the name Nankoweap is a bit of a mystery. Some scholars believe the word is derived from a Paiute phrase meaning "Place Where Two Tribes Fought." Others believe the phrase means "Place That Echoes." What is known is that Nankoweap was home to an Ancestral Puebloan settlement hundreds of years ago. These ancient people, predecessors of the modern Hopi and Navajo tribes, farmed the fertile delta at Nankoweap and built granaries (stone storage compartments) in the cliffs above.

> "And what a world of grandeur is spread before us! Below is the canyon through which the Colorado runs . . . Away to the west are lines of cliffs and ledges of rock—not such ledges as the reader may have seen where the quarry-man splits his blocks, but ledges from which the gods might quarry mountains . . ."
>
> —John Wesley Powell

Nankoweap

Trinity Canyon

Shinumo Creek

Elves Chasm

Blacktail Canyon

Deer Creek Falls

"The clouds are children of the heavens, and when they play among the rocks they lift them to the region above."

—John Wesley Powell

Deer Creek Narrows

Deer Creek Narrows

Kanab Canyon (river mile 143)

Kanab Canyon is one of Grand Canyon's largest and most beautiful side canyons. It was named by John Wesley Powell after the Paiute word for "willow." In 1872 Powell and his men ended their second Colorado River expedition here, hiking out of the canyon to the North Rim. One year earlier, two prospectors discovered trace amounts of gold in Kanab Canyon, setting off a minor gold rush that brought hundreds of fortune seekers. The gold rush, which lasted all of four months, ended when the eager prospectors reluctantly accepted that there were no sizeable gold deposits in Kanab Canyon.

"The crevices are usually narrow above and, by erosion of the streams, wider below, forming a network of caves, each cave having a narrow, winding skylight up through the rocks. Wherever we look there is but a wilderness of rocks—deep gorges where the rivers are lost below cliffs and towers and pinnacles, and ten thousand strangely carved forms in every direction . . ."

—John Wesley Powell

Havasu Canyon (river mile 157)

The beauty of Grand Canyon is stunning, but the beauty of Havasu Canyon seems almost hallucinatory. This secluded oasis—the most abundant side stream in Grand Canyon—is part lush paradise, part Southwestern dreamscape. A well-worn path heads up Havasu Canyon from the river, revealing shocking turquoise water tumbling over pink rocks in a series of tranquil pools, each more beautiful than the last. No matter how far up the path you go, you'll be greeted by some of the most incredible scenery in the Southwest.

Havasu Canyon is located on the Havasupai Indian Reservation. Follow the path up Havasu Canyon ten miles and you'll reach the village of Supai (p.291), home to about 400 members of the Havasupai tribe. *Havasupai*, loosely translated, means "People of the Blue-Green Water." Supai's world-famous waterfalls draw several thousand visitors a year, but the village, located 2,000 feet below the rim, is accessible only by foot, mule, or helicopter. It's unrealistic to hike from the river to Supai and back in a single day, but Beaver Falls (located about four miles up the trail) is a beautiful multi-tiered waterfall that makes a good destination for strong day hikers.

Havasu Canyon receives only nine inches of rain a year, but it drains a 3,000-square-mile basin. That drainage, combined with a gushing spring, provides Havasu Creek with an average of 38 million gallons of water a day. The vivid blue water is due to dissolved calcium carbonate and magnesium, which gives the water its otherworldly hue.

Beaver Falls, Havasu Canyon

National Canyon (river mile 166)

National Canyon is one of many exquisite side canyons branching off from the Colorado River. These canyons, carved over millions of years by flash floods roaring down from the rim, offer some of the most amazing scenery in Grand Canyon. Their walls have been sculpted and polished in an endless variety of patterns, alternately catching and concealing sunlight throughout the day. Many of these side canyons are accessible only from the river, making them the exclusive domain of river runners. Some go on for miles, offering incredible hiking that many river runners consider to be the best part of the trip.

> "The gorge is black and narrow below, red and gray and flaring above, with crags and angular projections on the walls, which, cut in many places by side canyons, seem to be a vast wilderness of rocks . . . and ever as we go there is some new pinnacle or tower, some crag or peak, some distant view of the upper plateau, some strangely shaped rock, or some deep, narrow side canyon."
>
> —John Wesley Powell

Matkatamiba Canyon

Matkatamiba Canyon

"What a conflict of water and fire there must have been here! Just imagine a river of molten rock running down into a river of melted snow. What a seething and boiling of the waters; what clouds of steam rolled into the heavens."

— John Wesley Powell

Lava Falls (river mile 179)

Lava Falls is one of the most challenging, terrifying, and thrilling rapids in Grand Canyon. It drops 13 feet in a matter of seconds, providing river runners with a rip-roaring ride, regardless of whether they stay inside the boat. Lava Falls is also the last major rapid conquered on most river trips—the grand finale after a symphony of singular sights.

Lava Falls is named for nearby lava flows. Over the past two million years, multiple volcanic eruptions have sent lava tumbling over the rim, which accounts for the dark-colored basalt on the north side of the river. Roughly 1.6 million years ago, a nearby volcanic eruption sent four cubic miles of lava tumbling down to the Colorado River. When the lava cooled, it plugged the canyon and formed a dam at least 2,300 feet high. This natural lava dam created a reservoir that took 22 years to fill and stretched hundreds of miles to Moab, Utah.

Lava Falls shows mercy to no man, as demonstrated in 1989, when the rapids flipped a boat carrying Hollywood heavyweights Tom Cruise and Jeffrey Katzenberg. In the late 1980s, private Grand Canyon "power trips" became popular among Tinseltown titans. The luxury on these trips was so extravagant, so over the top, so beyond anything Grand Canyon had ever seen that they are still talked about to this day. As the moguls conquered the rapids, extra supply rafts tagged along carrying gourmet food, wine, white linens, fine china, assistants, and private chefs. At night, candlelight dinners on the banks of the Colorado featured delicacies such as caviar and live lobster.

"Above and below us are cataracts where the water rushes with a deafening roar among huge blocks of basalt, and the voice of the waters is reverberated from the faces of the crags in a deep solemn monotone that never ceases."

—Clarence Dutton

Lava Falls

Cape Final

THE NORTH RIM

THE NORTH RIM lies just ten miles from the South Rim as the condor flies, but those of us confined to the ground have to drive 200 miles *around* Grand Canyon to get there. The closest major airport, McCarran in Las Vegas, is 280 miles to the southwest, and traveling to the North Rim means driving through one of the least densely populated places in the continental United States. As a result, fewer than one in ten Grand Canyon visitors makes it to the North Rim. But those who do are rewarded with reduced crowds and some of Grand Canyon's most spectacular scenery.

The North Rim is located 8,200 feet above sea level—over 1,000 feet higher than the South Rim. This results in cooler temperatures and 60 percent more precipitation. As a result, the North Rim is covered in alpine forests of spruce, fir, and aspen, giving it a feel more like the Rocky Mountains than the desert Southwest. During summer heat spells, when the South Rim is sweltering, the North Rim enjoys balmy afternoons and mild summer nights. Winters, on the other hand, bring so much snow that AZ-67—the only road to the North Rim—shuts down. Only cross-country skiers and snowshoers are allowed in the park during this time.

The hub of all activity on the North Rim is Grand Canyon Lodge, located at the southern terminus of AZ-67. The lodge offers overnight accommodations on the rim, but even if you're not a guest you can relax on the open-air back porch or dine in the upscale restaurant, both of which offer spectacular canyon views. A short distance away is the pristine North Rim Campground, which fills up fast in summer. Both the lodge and the campground are located within walking distance of Bright Angel Point, the North Rim's most popular overlook. A lazy drive along Cape Royal Road, meanwhile, brings you equally spectacular views at Point Imperial and Cape Royal on the Walhalla Plateau.

The North Rim doesn't have an extensive selection of restaurants or gift shops, but that's part of its charm. Visitors here are more interested in beautiful scenery and plentiful day hikes. If you're looking for a challenging overnight hike, the North Kaibab Trail (p.276) descends 14 miles to Bright Angel Campground and Phantom Ranch.

North Rim
BASICS

Getting to the North Rim

There's only one road to Grand Canyon's North Rim: AZ-67, which heads south from the small town of Jacob Lake off I-89A. From Jacob Lake follow AZ-67 roughly 44 miles south to the park entrance. From there it's an additional 13 miles to Grand Canyon Lodge. No trains or public buses go to the North Rim, but private shuttles make regular runs between the South Rim and the North Rim (see below). The closest major airports are located in Las Vegas (280 miles, 5 hours driving) and Salt Lake City (380 miles, 7 hours driving). A small regional airport is located in St. George, Utah (150 miles, 3 hours driving).

RIM TO RIM SHUTTLES

Trans-Canyon Shuttle (928-638-2820, trans-canyonshuttle.com) offers daily trips between the North Rim and the South Rim from May to October. The drive lasts about five hours each way. Cost: $90 per person, one-way.

Information

The best resource for North Rim information is the North Rim Visitor Center (open 8am–6pm), adjacent to Grand Canyon Lodge. It has a ranger-staffed help desk, maps, brochures, exhibits, and a well-stocked bookstore. The U.S. Forest Service also operates the Kaibab Plateau Visitor Center (open 8am–5pm) near the junction of I-89A and AZ-67.

Grand Canyon's free *Trip Planner*, which can be downloaded from the park website, offers basic North Rim information.

Fees

A seven-day pass to the North Rim (which includes access to the South Rim) costs $35 per vehicle, $30 per motorcycle, or $20 per pedestrian or cyclist. There's also an annual Grand Canyon Pass ($70). The best deal, however, is America the Beautiful Pass ($80), which gives you unlimited access to all U.S. national parks, national monuments, and federal recreation lands for one year.

Weather & When to Go

Winter dumps an average of 12 feet of snow on the North Rim, closing the park's only access road, AZ-67. The road reopens in spring when the snow melts, generally around mid-May. Spring is delightful, but the weather can be unpredictable. Pack warm clothes and be prepared for sudden temperature changes.

Summer is the busiest season on the North Rim, but crowds are rarely a problem. Due to its high elevation, the North Rim is about five to ten degrees cooler than the South Rim, which means summer temperatures are generally divine. But be prepared for regular afternoon thundershowers during "monsoon season," which lasts from July through early September.

Fall is a wonderful time on the North Rim, with sparse crowds and beautiful foliage, but prepare for cold temperatures at night. Although North Rim facilities shut down in mid-October, the park remains open until winter's first heavy snow, which often occurs around mid-November. When snowfall closes AZ-67, the park is only open to adventurous snowshoers and cross-country skiers.

What to Bring

Shopping at the North Rim is limited, so proper packing is essential. Make sure you bring plenty of warm clothes and rain gear. If you're camping, bring all the food and cooking equipment that you need. The North Rim's general store has a decent selection of food and camping equipment, but it sometimes run out of essentials during peak season.

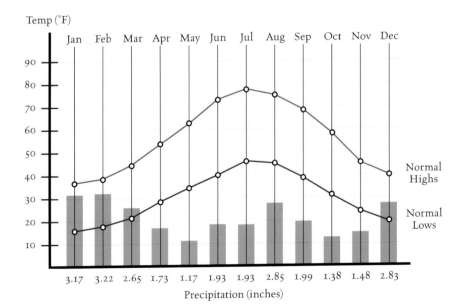

Getting Around the North Rim

It's possible to have a great time on the North Rim without your own set of wheels, but having a car or bike is essential if you want to explore the beautiful viewpoints not within walking distance of Grand Canyon Lodge. This includes the dramatic Walhalla Plateau (p.261), which offers some of the best viewpoints and day hikes on the North Rim.

Unlike the bustling South Rim, the North Rim does not offer regular shuttle service. The only shuttle on the North Rim is the early morning North Rim Hiker Shuttle, which runs between Grand Canyon Lodge and the North Kaibab Trailhead. The Hiker Shuttle picks up passengers in front of the lodge at 5:45am and 7:10am, May 15–October 15. Tickets are available at the front desk of the lodge. Reservations are required 24 hours in advance.

Note: bicycles are allowed on all paved and dirt roads on the North Rim, but they are prohibited from all other trails in the park. Bicycles are allowed on both the 1.2-mile Bridle Path and the 10-mile Arizona Trail.

Dining

★ THE LODGE DINING ROOM $$$ (Brk, Lnch, Din)

This grand restaurant offers the finest dining on the North Rim. The menu is a tasty mix of Western and Mediterranean classics. The atmosphere is rustic, and the canyon views are tremendous. Dinner reservations required (928-638-2612).

CHUCKWAGON BUFFET $$$ (Din)

This Western buffet at Grand Canyon Lodge offers prime rib, roasted pork, chicken, trout, veggies, and salad. Take your meal to the veranda and enjoy dinner with gorgeous canyon views.

DELI IN THE PINES $$$ (Lnch, Din)

Located on the west side of Grand Canyon Lodge, this cafeteria-style restaurant offers basic sandwiches, hot dogs, pizza, and a few healthy options like fresh fruits and salads. The interior is bland, so grab your food and head to one of the lodge's beautiful outdoor terraces.

ROUGH RIDER SALOON $$$ (Brk, Lnch, Din)

Early morning coffee shop by day, well-stocked bar by night. No matter when you visit, this classic saloon will transport you back to the rugged days of Teddy Roosevelt's Rough Riders. Pizza slices and light appetizers are available. Located on the east side of Grand Canyon Lodge.

Lodging

GRAND CANYON LODGE

Situated on the rim of Grand Canyon, this rustic lodge offers the North Rim's only overnight accommodations. Its motel-style rooms and rustic private cabins are generally booked a year in advance, but last-minute cancellations are sometimes available. Rates: $148–262 (877-386-4383, grandcanyonforever.com).

Camping

NORTH RIM CAMPGROUND

This beautiful, 90-site campground is located near the rim of the canyon. The best campsites with canyon views are 11, 14, 15, 16 and 18. Rates: $18 per night, $25 for sites with canyon views. Visitors without cars pay $4 per night for campsites with canyon views. Reservations, which can be made up to six months in advance, are highly recommended. (877-444-6777, recreation.gov)

Gas, Groceries & Services

Just past the turnoff to the North Rim Campground there's a gas station with 24-hour pumps. Continue down the road to a shower house with coin-operated showers and laundry on your right. Just beyond the shower house, next to the campground entrance, is the North Rim General Store, which sells basic groceries, beer, wine, and camping supplies.

Activities

RANGER PROGRAMS

Free ranger programs are one of the best ways to learn about Grand Canyon. Popular topics including history, geology, and wildlife. Inquire at visitor centers for seasonal times and locations.

MULE RIDES

Don't feel like hiking? You can ride a mule along the rim or partway down the North Kaibab Trail. One-hour trips ($45) and three-hour trips ($90) are available (435-679-8665, canyonrides.com).

SPECIAL EVENTS

Each June the North Rim hosts the **Grand Canyon Star Party**; dates vary depending on the new moon. **Western Arts Day** celebrates Arizona and Utah's Western heritage in mid-July. **American Indian Heritage Days**, which celebrates Grand Canyon's native tribes (p.74), is held in early August. **Symphony of the Canyon** brings musicians together for open-air concerts in August.

OUTSIDE THE PARK

AZ-67, which connects the tiny town of Jacob Lake to the North Rim, has a handful of lodges, campgrounds, and restaurants. Visit jameskaiser.com for more info on lodging and camping outside the North Rim.

Kaibab National Forest

Much of Grand Canyon's North Rim is part of Kaibab National Forest. A spider web of dirt roads leads through the forest, some to fabulous viewpoints and hiking trails. Dispersed camping is permitted. For more information swing by the Kaibab Plateau Visitor Center in Jacob Lake or visit fs.usda.gov.

Lodging

KAIBAB LODGE

Located six miles north of the park entrance, these cabins are a good alternative to Grand Canyon Lodge. Rates: $100-185 (928-638-2389, kaibablodge.com).

JACOB LAKE INN

Located 31 miles north of the park entrance, the Jacob Lake Inn offers both motel rooms and private cabins. Rates: $102-165 (928-643-7232, jacoblake.com).

North Rim Bison

Between Grand Canyon's North Rim and Jacob Lake, Highway 67 passes a series of beautiful meadows where bison sometimes graze. Standing six feet tall and weighing 2,000 pounds or more, bison are the largest land-dwelling mammals in North America. But these majestic animals are not native to the Kaibab Plateau. They were brought here in the early 1900s by a rancher who wanted to crossbreed them with cattle to make "cattalo." The attempt failed, but the bison remained, and eventually a large herd roamed the Kaibab National Forest. For decades hunting kept their population in check, until the bison realized they were protected in Grand Canyon National Park, where hunting is illegal. Today roughly 400 to 600 bison live year-round in the park. Unfortunately, the bison threaten fragile ecosystems, and their numbers continue to grow. As a result, the National Park Service is actively trying to reduce the size of the herd.

Camping

DEMOTTE CAMPGROUND

This 38-site campground is located six miles north of the park entrance in the Kaibab National Forest. Cost: $22 per night. (877-444-6777, recreation.gov)

JACOB LAKE CAMPGROUND

This 51-site campground is located 31 miles north of the park entrance in Jacob Lake. Cost: $22 per night. (877-444-6777, recreation.gov)

Dining

JACOB LAKE INN $$$ (Brk, Lnch, Din)

Hearty food in a cozy atmosphere. Try the Kaibab Jagerschnitzel, a pork cutlet grilled with bacon and juniper berries. (928-643-7232)

KAIBAB LODGE RESTAURANT $$$ (Brk, Lnch, Din)

This rustic restaurant serves breakfast classics, sandwiches, burgers, soups, and steaks. Located six miles north of the park entrance on AZ-67. (928-638-2389)

Gas & Supplies

Jacob Lake has 24-hour gas pumps, and the Jacob Lake Inn has a small store with homemade baked goods. About 25 miles south of Jacob Lake is the North Rim Country Store, which sells basic groceries, beer, firewood, and gas.

Kanab, Utah

This small town (population 5,000) is a great place to stay if you can't find loding or camping near the North Rim. There are plenty of hotels and restaurants, and the 1.5-hour drive from Kanab to the North Rim is beautiful.

WILLOW CANYON OUTDOOR

Outdoor enthusiasts flock to this charming gear shop/cafe/bookstore. Stock up for your next adventure, or simply kick back and relax with an espresso and a good book. (263 South 100 East, 435-644-8884)

RED PUEBLO MUSEUM

Located just north of Fredonia, the Red Pueblo Museum displays a remarkable collection of Ancestral Puebloan and native artifacts. Museum founder Dixon Spendlove offers fascinating tours. (1140 N Hwy 89A, 928-643-7777)

STAR PARTY TONIGHT

Kanab's dark skies are perfect for stargazing. This nightly astronomy program reveals the wonders of the universe. (kanabstars.com)

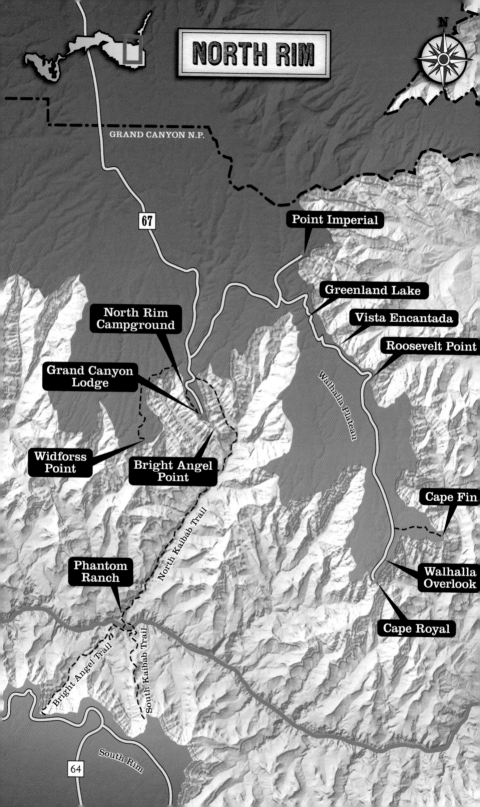

Bright Angel Point

This popular viewpoint, located 0.5 miles southeast of Grand Canyon Lodge, is accessible via a short paved path that begins to the left of the North Rim Visitor Center (just beyond the cabin area). After an initial drop, the trail stays relatively flat with only a few mild ups and downs. Dramatic views of Roaring Springs Canyon unfold to your left. Towards the end of the trail you'll cross a small bridge that takes you to the viewpoint.

Rising 8,148 feet above sea level, Bright Angel Point is fenced in by a small metal railing. Interpretive signs point out famous canyon landmarks visible in the distance. The rocky outcrop directly behind the observation platform is a popular place to take in the view, but use caution if you scamper on the rocks.

Gazing across Grand Canyon from Bright Angel Point, the walls of the South Rim appear nearly vertical. The walls of the North Rim, meanwhile, gradually recede from the Colorado River. This stark contrast is due to varying rates of erosion. Both the North Rim and the South Rim are tilted slightly to the south, so any precipitation that falls on the North Rim flows *into* the canyon, while any precipitation that falls on the South Rim flows *away* from the canyon. Because the walls of the North Rim receive so much more runoff, they erode horizontally up to ten times faster than the walls of the South Rim.

Beyond the South Rim, dotting the southeastern horizon, are the San Francisco Peaks (p.104). On clear days you can see Humphrey's Peak, the highest point in Arizona (12,643 feet).

Grand Canyon Lodge

Perched right on the rim, Grand Canyon Lodge offers tremendous views of the canyon from its two open-air terraces. During the day, these terraces are great places to enjoy the views (and a cocktail). At night, a fire often crackles in the stone fireplace on the eastern terrace. Sandwiched between the terraces is the indoor Sun Room, where comfy leather chairs face giant picture windows. The Sun Room is a great place to watch thunderstorms during monsoon season. There's a bronze statue of Brighty the Mule (rub his nose for good luck) and a large Hopi Kachina (p.92) over the fireplace. Several beautiful Navajo rugs are also draped around the lodge.

The original Grand Canyon Lodge, built in 1928, was the brainchild of Stephen Mather, the first director of the National Park Service. In the 1920s Mather championed the construction of grand lodges in national parks. Beautiful lodges helped lure visitors to national parks, which, in turn, helped justify the existence of the fledgling National Park Service. Designed by Gilbert Stanley Underwood— the architect behind Yosemite's famous Ahwahnee Hotel—the original Grand Canyon Lodge was built out of native ponderosa pine and Kaibab limestone. But just four years after it opened, the original structure burned down. Only the small buildings on either side of the structure were spared, and they are still in use today. A rebuilt lodge opened in 1936. When completed it boasted improvements such as steel beams (as opposed to flammable pine beams) and sloped roofs to deflect the North Rim's heavy snow.

Summer monsoon viewed from Grand Canyon Lodge

"It seems a gigantic statement for even nature to make, all in one mighty stone word, apprehended at once like a burst of light ... Wildness so godful, cosmic, primeval, bestows a new sense of earth's beauty and size."
—John Muir

Point Imperial

At 8,803 feet, Point Imperial is the highest viewpoint in Grand Canyon National Park. Its eastern exposure also makes it the North Rim's best place to watch sunrise. To get there from Grand Canyon Lodge, drive three miles north on AZ-67, then turn right onto Cape Royal Road. After 5.4 miles the road forks. Turn left onto Point Imperial Road, which ends at a large parking area with picnic tables and restrooms. Park your car and walk down to the dramatic viewpoint below.

The prominent spire in front of Point Imperial is the top of Mount Hayden (8,372 feet). The spire is composed of Coconino Sandstone, the third-youngest rock layer in Grand Canyon, which formed 265 million years ago when northern Arizona was covered with massive sand dunes similar to today's Sahara Desert. Over millions of years, those sand dunes were buried and compressed into sandstone. So when you look at Mount Hayden, you're actually looking at the compressed remains of 265-million-year-old sand dunes!

Beyond Mount Hayden the view stretches for miles, offering one of the best panoramas in the park. Left of Mount Hayden the Colorado River flows through Marble Canyon (p.214) before reaching the confluence of the Little Colorado River (look for a deep side canyon slicing through the east rim). Above Marble Canyon a broad, flat platform marks the westernmost edge of the Painted Desert, which stretches 150 miles southeast to Petrified Forest National Park. Almost all visible land east of Marble Canyon belongs to the Navajo Nation, whose 27,425-square-mile reservation is the largest in the U.S.

Vista Encantada

Walhalla Plateau

This dramatic "sky peninsula" juts 15 miles into Grand Canyon east of Grand Canyon Lodge. Thanks to warm updrafts on three sides, Walhalla Plateau has a relatively warm climate despite its 8,000-foot elevation. A 14.5-mile road heads to the plateau's southern tip, passing beautiful viewpoints and great day hikes along the way. To get there drive three miles north from Grand Canyon Lodge, then turn right onto Cape Royal Road. When the road forks after 5.4 miles, turn right and head south.

About 2.5 miles past the junction there's a small parking area next to Greenland Lake. This limestone sinkhole is a rare example of standing water on the rim of Grand Canyon, and dozens of prehistoric hunting artifacts have been found nearby. Continue along Cape Royal Road to Vista Encantada ("Enchanting View"). At 8,480 feet above sea level, it offers beautiful views of eastern Grand Canyon and the Painted Desert beyond. Two miles down the road is Roosevelt Point (8,470 feet). A 0.2-mile trail loops through the woods near Roosevelt Point, offering lovely canyon views. Past Roosevelt Point the road continues 5.5 miles through the forest to the start of Cape Final (p.270), a two-mile trail to one of the North Rim's most spectacular viewpoints.

From the Cape Final trailhead it's one mile to Walhalla Overlook and Walhalla Glades (p.262). The road ends at Cape Royal (p.265), which offers some of the North Rim's best sunset views.

Walhalla Glades

Walhalla Overlook

This gorgeous overlook (elevation: 7,998 feet) offers some of the best views on the Walhalla Plateau. From the rim a rugged side canyon tumbles down to Unkar Creek, which flows to Unkar Delta on the Colorado River. Around A.D. 1100, Unkar Delta was home to one of the largest known Ancestral Puebloan communities in Grand Canyon. As many as ten families may have called this area home. In winter they farmed the fertile delta. In summer they migrated to the Walhalla Plateau, where warm updrafts melt snow sooner than in other parts of the North Rim. Farmers captured snowmelt in irrigation systems to grow beans, corn, and squash. All told, over 100 ancient farm sites have been identified on the Walhalla Plateau. It's possible that population growth at Unkar Delta led to food shortages, driving farmers to the North Rim in search of fertile soil.

Across the road from Walhalla Overlook lies Walhalla Glades, the North Rim's most accessible archaeological ruin. Crumbling stone foundations mark the outline of a nine-room building used by Ancestral Puebloans 900 years ago. For roughly 100 years, as many as 20 people made Walhalla Glades their summer home. Large rooms were probably living quarters, while smaller rooms were used for storage. Additional storage rooms were located in a 15-room structure located on top of a rugged "sky island" visible from Walhalla Overlook. Why ancient farmers decided to build this storage space in such a difficult-to-reach place is a mystery. Some archaeologists speculate that it could be an indication of conflict between neighboring groups fighting over limited resources.

Desert View
Watchtower

Unkar Delta

Walhalla Overlook

Angels Window

Cape Royal

Cape Royal Road ends at a large parking area at the southern tip of the plateau. From the parking area, a paved 0.3-mile path heads through pinyon pines to Angels Window, a natural stone arch that frames a view of the Colorado River. When the path forks, turn left to walk onto the flat platform directly above Angels Window. You'll enjoy panoramic views north and east.

For most visitors, however, the real highlight is Cape Royal, which is reached by turning right at the fork. At 7,865 feet above sea level, Cape Royal offers exceptional views south towards the widest part of Grand Canyon. Directly in front of the viewpoint, sheer sandstone cliffs wrap around Wotans Throne, a wooded mesa partially detached from Cape Royal. Although seemingly inaccessible, a "Lost World Expedition" from the American Museum of Natural History scaled Wotans Throne in the 1930s. Their purpose: to determine if the isolated "sky island" contained animals unknown to science. No dinosaurs were found, but the expedition did discover archaeological evidence that native tribes spent time on Wotans Throne.

Sunset Tip!

If the crowds are big at Cape Royal, head to the little-known "Wedding Area" off the southwestern end of the parking area. This beautiful viewpoint, which accommodates weddings of up to 40 people, has equally impressive views with a fraction of the crowds—unless someone's getting hitched.

❧ TRANSEPT TRAIL ↶

SUMMARY The Transept Trail is an easy stroll through ponderosa pine forest between Grand Canyon Lodge and North Rim Campground. Along the way, the trail skirts the rim of Transept Canyon, treating hikers to dramatic views. Benches are set up at good vantage points, offering views of Bright Angel Point, the South Rim, and the San Francisco Peaks beyond. Along the way to the campground, you'll pass the stone remains of a two-room house occupied by Ancestral Puebloans roughly 900 years ago. In the early morning the Transept Trail is a great place to see wildlife such as mule deer, chipmunks, and squirrels. Bird watchers should keep an eye out for wrens, juncos, and woodpeckers. Consider looping back on the Bridle Path (3.6 miles round-trip), which offers good views of Roaring Springs Canyon.

TRAILHEAD From Grand Canyon Lodge: head down the obvious trail towards Bright Angel Point and turn right off the pavement after one-tenth of a mile. From North Rim Campground: head west from the general store and look for the sign that marks the trail.

◀ TRAIL INFO ▶

RATING: Easy

DISTANCE: 2 miles, one-way

HIKING TIME: 1 hour

ELEVATION CHANGE: 100 feet

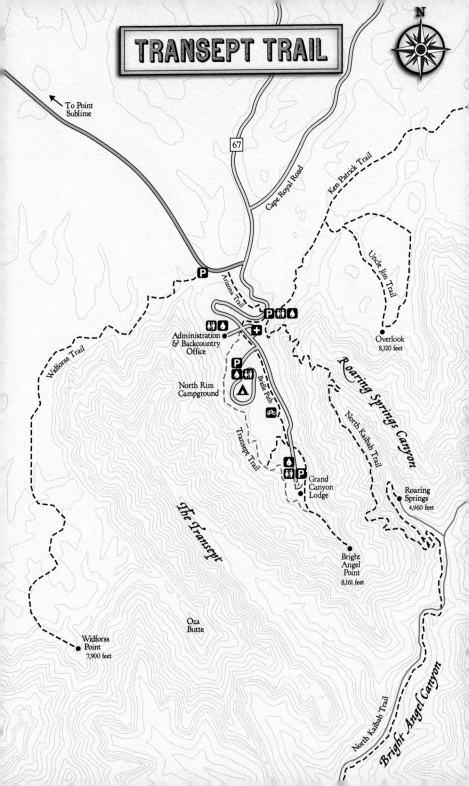

⊷ UNCLE JIM TRAIL ⟡

SUMMARY   This charming hike passes through the forest above Roaring Springs Canyon to a dramatic viewpoint. In spring you'll enjoy beautiful wild-flowers; in autumn golden aspen trees light up the trail. The only drawback: mule riders use the Uncle Jim Trail 7:30–10:30am and 12:30–3:30pm. Try timing your hike so you're not at the viewpoint around 9am or 2pm when the mules are there. To get to the Uncle Jim Loop, follow the Ken Patrick Trail 0.9 miles, then turn right at the junction. After 0.3 miles you'll reach another junction. I like bear-ing left, following the loop clockwise to better enjoy the canyon views as you approach the viewpoint. You'll know you're close when you see metal hitching posts. Beyond the hitching posts a narrow path twists through shrubs to the viewpoint. Standing high above Bright Angel Canyon, you'll enjoy dramatic views of enormous rock formations tumbling towards the South Rim. On clear days the San Francisco Peaks pierce the horizon.

TRAILHEAD   The hike to the Uncle Jim Loop starts at the Ken Patrick trailhead, two miles north of Grand Canyon Lodge next to the North Kaibab trailhead.

◆ TRAIL INFO ◆

RATING: Moderate   **HIKING TIME:** 3 hours

DISTANCE: 5 miles, round-trip   **ELEVATION CHANGE:** 230 feet

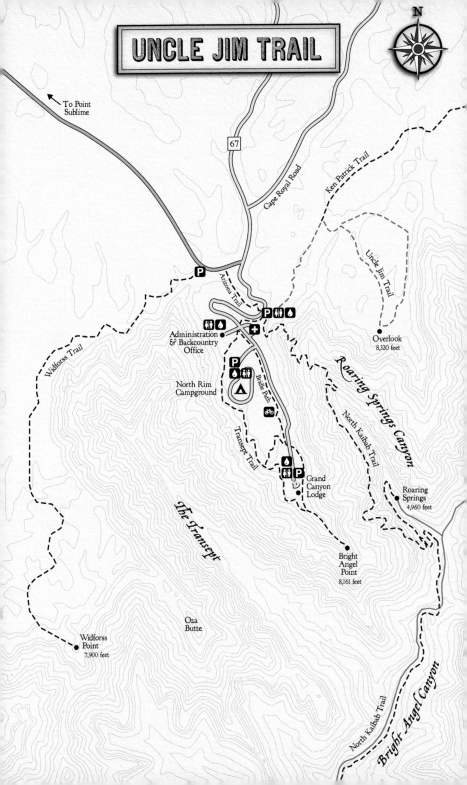

ᘒ CAPE FINAL TRAIL ᕬ

SUMMARY   This highly recommended hike heads to the easternmost tip of Walhalla Plateau, offering sweeping views of Vishnu Temple, Jupiter Temple, and eastern Grand Canyon. The views are among the finest on the North Rim, and due to Cape Final's relatively remote location there are rarely crowds. From Cape Royal Road, the trail heads through an open ponderosa forest, then winds past cacti and pinyon pines as you approach the rim. Cape Final, which is reached via a faint path, can be a bit hard to find. Look for the USGS datum points embedded in the bedrock at the overlook. Backpacking note: it's possible to camp at Cape Final. The park's Backcountry Office grants one camping permit per night. If you're lucky enough to get your hands on that permit, you'll have Cape Final all to yourself at night!

TRAILHEAD   The Cape Final Trail starts along Cape Royal Road. The small trailhead (which can be easy to miss) starts roughly 11.8 miles south of the junction with Point Imperial Road (2.5 miles north of the end of Cape Royal Road).

◆ TRAIL INFO ◆

RATING: Easy

DISTANCE: 4 miles, round-trip

HIKING TIME: 2 hours

ELEVATION CHANGE: 150 feet

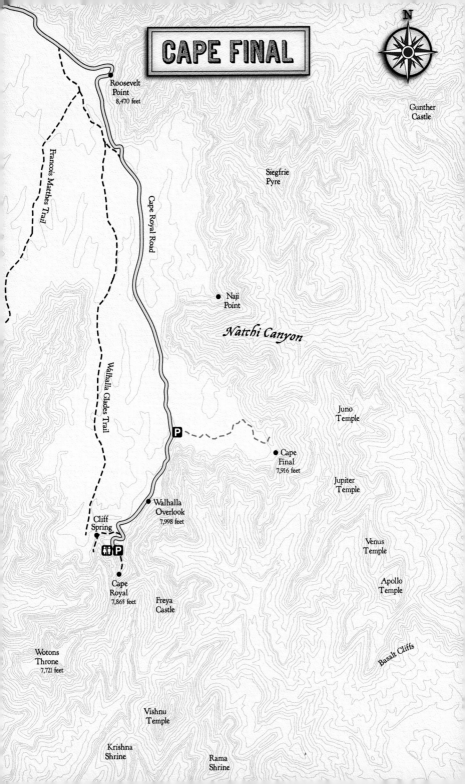

CAPE FINAL

N

Roosevelt
Point
8,470 feet

Gunther
Castle

Francois Matthes Trail

Siegfrie
Pyre

Cape Royal Road

Naji
Point

Natchi Canyon

Walhalla Glades Trail

Juno
Temple

P

Cape Final
7,916 feet

Jupiter
Temple

Walhalla
Overlook
7,998 feet

Venus
Temple

Cliff
Spring

P

Apollo
Temple

Cape
Royal
7,865 feet

Freya
Castle

Wotons
Throne
7,721 feet

Basalt Cliffs

Vishnu
Temple

Krishna
Shrine

Rama
Shrine

◄ CLIFF SPRING TRAIL ►

SUMMARY This easy trail, located near the southern tip of the Walhalla Plateau, rambles along a steep, forested ravine to a small spring. About 100 yards past the trailhead there's an Ancestral Puebloan granary, which was used roughly 1,000 years ago to store crops. Beyond the granary, the trail drops down and wraps around striking 30-foot cliffs with a pronounced overhang. Soon you'll reach a peaceful rock alcove filled with moss, ferns, and other vegetation. Look close and you can see Cliff Spring dripping from the rock into small, shallow pools. (Note: do not drink the water, which may be contaminated.) A rugged trail continues past Cliff Spring, providing dramatic views as the steep ravine plummets into Grand Canyon.

TRAILHEAD The Cliff Spring Trail starts on the inside of a hairpin turn about half a mile from the end of Cape Royal Road (roughly 13.5 miles south of the junction with Point Imperial Road). Parking is available at a pullover on the left side of the road. A signed trailhead is located across the street.

TRAIL INFO

RATING: Easy

DISTANCE: 1 mile, round-trip

HIKING TIME: 1 hour

ELEVATION CHANGE: 200 feet

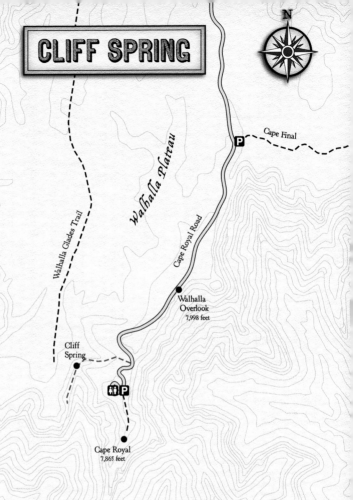

CLIFF SPRING

N

Walhalla Plateau

Walhalla Glades Trail

Cape Royal Road

P Cape Final

Walhalla Overlook
7,998 feet

Cliff Spring

Cape Royal
7,865 feet

Freya Castle

Wotans Throne
7,721 feet

Vishnu Temple

⊰ WIDFORSS TRAIL ⊱

SUMMARY   This long hike skirts the edge of Transept Canyon, then cuts through the forest to Widforss Point. For lovers of wildflowers and woodland scenery, the Widforss Trail has few rivals on the North Rim. After a quick climb at the start, the trail skirts the forested rim. Numbered posts correspond to points of interest listed in a brochure available at the trailhead. Eventually the trail veers away from the rim and heads through the forest. The trail narrows towards the end, reaching an old picnic table before dropping to Widforss Point, which offers panoramic canyon views. Both Widforss Point and the Widforss Trail were named in honor of artist Gunnar M. Widforss, who painted vivid watercolors of Grand Canyon in the 1930s. Backpacking note: camping permits are available for the Widforss Trail.

TRAILHEAD   From Grand Canyon Lodge, drive north on AZ-67 for about 2.5 miles until you see a sign for the turnoff to Widforss Point. Turn left onto the dirt road and follow it for about half a mile. There is a signed parking area for the Widforss Trail on the left. The trail starts on the south side of the parking area.

◀ TRAIL INFO ▶

RATING: Moderate

HIKING TIME: 4–5 hours

DISTANCE: 10 miles, round-trip

ELEVATION CHANGE: 400 feet

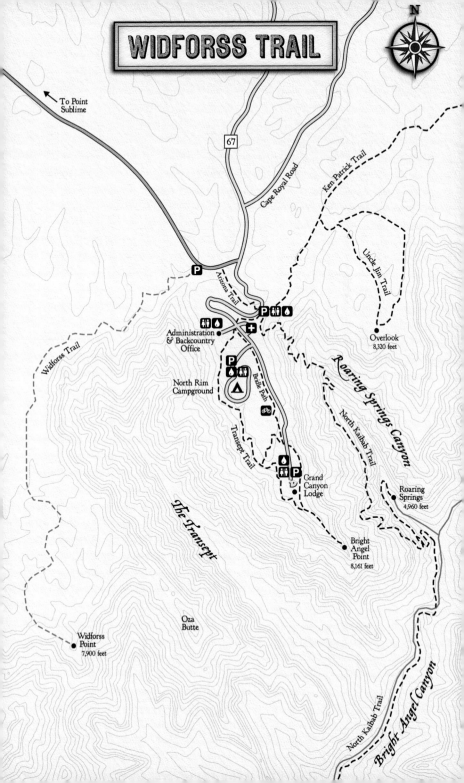

❧ NORTH KAIBAB TRAIL ❧

SUMMARY   The steep, strenuous North Kaibab Trail is the only maintained trail on the North Rim that descends into Grand Canyon. Though physically demanding, it's one of the best hikes in the park, passing through an incredible range of ecological zones. Backpackers typically spend three to four days hiking the trail, spending the night at Cottonwood Campground (halfway down the trail) and Bright Angel Campground (located near the Colorado River). Day hikers can head to Coconino Overlook (1.5 miles, round-trip) or Supai Tunnel (4 miles, round-trip). Two beautiful waterfalls, Roaring Springs and Ribbon Falls, are accessible via short side trails much farther down the trail. Towards the end of the North Kaibab Trail, you'll pass through The Box—a narrow, shady corridor that twists along Bright Angel Creek through 1.7-billion-year-old Vishnu Schist.

TRAILHEAD   The trail starts about two miles north of Grand Canyon Lodge just off AZ-67. A small parking area is located next to the trailhead. There's also a free early morning shuttle that departs from Grand Canyon Lodge (p.256).

TRAIL INFO

RATING: Strenuous   **HIKING TIME:** 3–4 Days

DISTANCE: 28 miles, round-trip   **ELEVATION CHANGE:** 5,850 feet

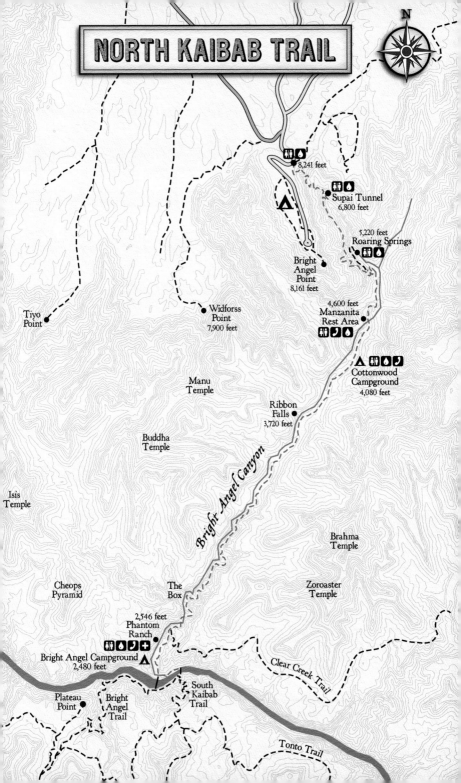

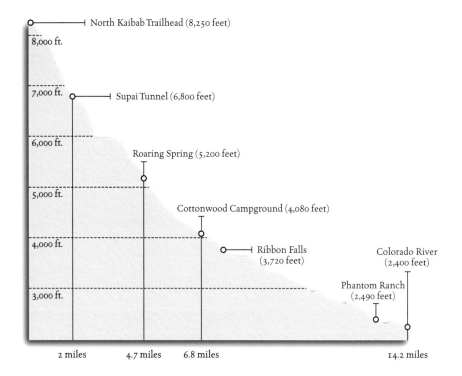

North Kaibab Trailhead (8,250 feet)

8,000 ft.

7,000 ft.   Supai Tunnel (6,800 feet)

6,000 ft.

Roaring Spring (5,200 feet)

5,000 ft.

Cottonwood Campground (4,080 feet)

4,000 ft.

Ribbon Falls
(3,720 feet)

Colorado River
(2,400 feet)

Phantom Ranch
(2,490 feet)

3,000 ft.

2 miles   4.7 miles   6.8 miles   14.2 miles

NORTH KAIBAB TRAIL

Ribbon Falls

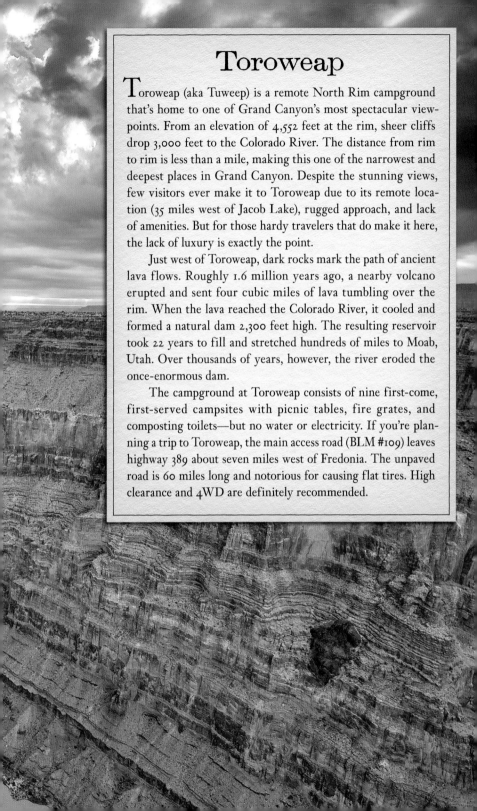

Toroweap

Toroweap (aka Tuweep) is a remote North Rim campground that's home to one of Grand Canyon's most spectacular viewpoints. From an elevation of 4,552 feet at the rim, sheer cliffs drop 3,000 feet to the Colorado River. The distance from rim to rim is less than a mile, making this one of the narrowest and deepest places in Grand Canyon. Despite the stunning views, few visitors ever make it to Toroweap due to its remote location (35 miles west of Jacob Lake), rugged approach, and lack of amenities. But for those hardy travelers that do make it here, the lack of luxury is exactly the point.

Just west of Toroweap, dark rocks mark the path of ancient lava flows. Roughly 1.6 million years ago, a nearby volcano erupted and sent four cubic miles of lava tumbling over the rim. When the lava reached the Colorado River, it cooled and formed a natural dam 2,300 feet high. The resulting reservoir took 22 years to fill and stretched hundreds of miles to Moab, Utah. Over thousands of years, however, the river eroded the once-enormous dam.

The campground at Toroweap consists of nine first-come, first-served campsites with picnic tables, fire grates, and composting toilets—but no water or electricity. If you're planning a trip to Toroweap, the main access road (BLM #109) leaves highway 389 about seven miles west of Fredonia. The unpaved road is 60 miles long and notorious for causing flat tires. High clearance and 4WD are definitely recommended.

Havasu Falls

HAVASU CANYON

To GRAND CANYON visitors in the know, the word Havasu conjures images of a remote desert paradise. Located about 35 miles west of Grand Canyon Village, Havasu Canyon is one of the most beautiful destinations in the Southwest. For over 700 years, Grand Canyon's largest side canyon has been home to the Havasupai, "People of the Blue-Green Water," who derive their name from the vibrant turquoise stream that flows through Havasu Canyon. Today over 400 Havasupai live in the tiny village of Supai, located 2,000 feet below the rim. A short distance from the village are Havasu Falls and Mooney Falls—two of the most stunning waterfalls in America.

Although Havasu Canyon receives an average of just nine inches of rain each year, a natural spring near Supai releases 40 million gallons of water a day. The color of the water, an electric blue more typical of the Caribbean than the desert Southwest, is due to natural minerals dissolved in the water. As Havasu Creek flows down the red rock canyon, it tumbles over dozens of beautiful pools and cascades. The creek also supports a lush riparian habitat of cottonwood trees, maidenhair fern, and scarlet monkey flowers.

Is Havasu Canyon too good to be true? Almost. Due to its rugged, remote location, getting here is a bit of a challenge. Hualapai Hilltop, the jumping-off point for the eight-mile hike into the canyon, is reached after a long drive along desolate roads. From the hilltop it's an eight-mile hike into Havasu Canyon. No roads lead to Supai, which is the last town in the United States where daily mail is delivered by mule.

Also, all Havasu visitors must have camping or lodging reservations to enter the canyon. For decades Havasu Canyon was something of a local secret. But global interest has exploded in recent years, driven largely by social media. When reservations open for the year, they often sell out within hours. The hardest part about visiting Havasu Canyon used to be the physical challenge of getting there. Now it's simply getting a reservation.

Because Havasu Canyon remains isolated from much of the outside world, the pace of life here is distinctly different. The Havasupai continue to speak their native language, horses and dogs freely roam the dirt roads, and illumination is mostly provided by the sun and the moon. All this, combined with breathtaking natural scenery, makes Havasu Canyon one of America's most fascinating destinations.

Basic Info

Thanks to the post-Instagram surge in visitation, fees and reservations have recently been in a state of flux. For the most up-to-date Havasu Canyon info, check the Havasupai Tribe's official website: theofficialhavasupaitribe.com.

Rules & Regulations

All visitors must have advance reservations at either the campground or lodge, or they will not be allowed to enter Havasu Canyon. Among the many things not permitted in Havasu Canyon: alcohol, smoking, drones, jumping/diving into pools, amplified music, campfires, inner tubes, pool toys, and nudity.

Getting to Havasu Canyon

Havasu Canyon is just 35 miles west of Grand Canyon Village as the condor flies, but it's about 200 miles away by road. The trail to the village of Supai starts at Hualapai Hilltop, on the rim of Havasu Canyon. To get there from Grand Canyon Village, take I-40 to the town of Seligman, then turn onto AZ-66 heading toward Peach Springs. A little under 30 miles past Seligman (six miles east of Peach Springs), turn onto Indian Route Highway 18 and follow it roughly 60 miles to Hualapai Hilltop.

Hiking into Havasu Canyon

The trail to Supai is eight miles long and descends 2,000 vertical feet. Plan on roughly four hours hiking down and five hours hiking up. There are some challenging switchbacks near the top, but the majority of the trail is a moderate hike. The best seasons to hike are spring and fall. Be aware that midday summer temperatures can top 115°F. Try to hike in the morning, when temperatures are cooler. No matter when you go, carry at least one gallon of water per person. Note: the campground is an additional two miles past Supai. If you don't want to carry your camping gear, you can arrange to have your gear carried down by pack mule.

Havasupai Lodge

The two-story Havasupai Lodge offers 24 motel-style rooms with air conditioning and private bathrooms. There's no TV, but there is mobile phone service. As of this writing, Havasu Lodge reservations are available only by phone (928-448-2111 or 928-448-2201). Reservations become available on June 1 for the following year, and they sell out fast. Cancellations are sometimes available. Rates: $440 per room/per night, with up to four people per room. There's also a $110 per person entrance/environmental fee.

Camping

A large campground is located two miles north of Supai along Havasu Stream. Reservations for the 350 spots are *extremely* competitive. As of this writing, the online reservation system (havasupaireservations.com) opens for the year on February 1, and most spots sell out within a few hours. To increase your chances of getting a reservation, create an account before February 1. Then log in the morning of February 1 and pray. All campsite reservations are for a minimum of three nights. Cost: $100/night Monday through Thursday, $125/night Friday through Sunday.

Pack Mules

For $400, a mule will carry your gear between the Hualapai Hilltop and the Havasu Canyon campground. One mule can carry up to four bags. Maximum weight: 32 pounds per bag. Maximum bag size: 36 x 19 x 19 inches. Pack mule reservations are available at havasupaireservations.com.

Food & Dining

There's only one restaurant in Supai: the Tribal Cafe, which serves cafeteria-style food (try the Indian taco) with a few vegetarian options. The cafe is generally open 8am–5pm, but hours vary (928-448-2981). There's also a small grocery store across from the cafe that sells basic goods. Some Havasu families run small stores and restaurants out of their homes (look for signs as you stroll through town).

Lodging Near Hualapai Hilltop

Driving to Hualapai Hilltop from Grand Canyon Village, Flagstaff, or Williams takes several hours. After a long drive, the last thing you want to do is start the long journey into Havasu Canyon. A better option is spending the night at one of the nearby hotels along AZ-66, then getting an early start the next morning. This is especially true in the hot summer months, when morning shade provides relief from the scorching sun.

GRAND CANYON CAVERNS INN

This basic 48-room motel, located along a lonely stretch of Route 66, offers the closest lodging to Hualapai Hilltop. It's situated on top of a large cave system. Tours of the caves are available, and there's even a giant "Cavern Suite" located 220 feet underground (928-422-3223, gccaverns.com).

HUALAPAI LODGE

This modern 60-room hotel, located in the small town of Peach Springs, is a step up from Grand Canyon Caverns Inn, but you'll have to drive a few extra miles to Hualapai Hilltop (928-769-2636, grandcanyonwest.com).

HISTORY

GENETIC EVIDENCE INDICATES the Havasupai are descended from the first wave of human migrants to enter North America roughly 15,000 years ago. The Havasupai refer to themselves as *Havsuw 'Baaja* ("People of the Blue-Green Water"). Havasupai creation myths speak of a time when Coyote and other animal gods imparted their wisdom to the tribe, establishing their basic customs and rituals. Archaeological evidence indicates that Havasu Canyon has been occupied for at least 700 years.

In summer, the Havasupai historically tended gardens of beans, corn, and squash. Their irrigation techniques, which may have come from Mexico, were among the most advanced in the Southwest. In addition to Havasu Canyon, the Havasupai farmed several side canyons along Grand Canyon's South Rim, including Indian Gardens below present-day Grand Canyon Village. Dozens of wild plants such as agave and pinyon pine provided additional food.

Havasu Canyon is the tribe's most important location, but their territory covered a vast area along much of Grand Canyon's South Rim. In winter, when the sun shines only a few hours in Havasu Canyon each day, the tribe moved to open plateaus along the South Rim. Snow provided a steady source of water, firewood was abundant, and rabbit and deer supplemented their diet.

Daily life revolved around farming, food gathering, hunting, cooking, tool-making, and socializing. Social conformity was extremely important, and members of the tribe who didn't follow traditional Havasupai ways were shamed and ostracized. Women were often treated as property, and polygamy was practiced by high-status males, but there was no formal marriage ceremony. After a male suitor gave sufficient gifts to an unmarried girl's family, the couple were considered married.

Traditional Havasupai dwellings consisted of earth-covered conical huts with dirt floors. Clothes, moccasins, and blankets were fashioned from animal hides. Women often wore face paint and jewelry, and important ceremonies featured elaborate costumes and body paint.

The Havasupai had friendly relations with the neighboring Hopi and Navajo tribes. The three tribes often gathered at annual celebrations with feasting, dancing, and gambling. During these gatherings, the Havasupai traded vegetables and buckskin for jewelry and blankets.

Not all neighboring tribes had friendly relations with the Havasupai. The Yavapai and Paiute occasionally carried out violent raids in Havasu Canyon. To defend their territory, the Havasupai retreated to high cliffs, where they shot arrows poisoned with toxic liquids from plants and scorpions. Another favorite battle tactic was rolling heavy rocks down on the invaders.

Following the Spanish colonization of North America, the Havasupai acquired horses. They also added melons, peaches, and pears to their gardens.

Due to their remote location, however, they had little direct contact with the Spanish, and their lifestyle was far less impacted than those of other tribes. In the mid-1800s, white miners and ranchers arrived in northern Arizona, and land conflicts with the Havasupai ensued. In 1882 the federal government ordered the Havasupai onto a reservation in Havasu Canyon less than one square mile in size. A separate reservation was set up for the Hualapai ("Pine Tree People") on the rim. Forced onto separate reservations, the Havasupai and Hualapai, who previously considered themselves part of the same tribe, became two distinct tribes. In a further blow to the Havasupai, the government denied them access to their traditional winter hunting grounds on the rim. Confined to a tiny reservation with barely enough land to feed themselves, and ravaged by previously unknown European diseases, the Havasupai population plummeted.

Meanwhile, as more and more manufactured goods trickled into the region, the Havasupai abandoned many of their traditional ways. Cotton shirts replaced animal skins, rifles replaced bows and arrows, and pottery making was abandoned. Despite the changes, the Havasupai retained far more of their culture than many other tribes. In the 1930s, an anthropologist visiting Supai remarked that it was "the only spot in the United States where native culture has remained in anything like its pristine condition." As the decades wore on, however, the Havasupai continued to suffer. Alcohol and diabetes added to the tribe's growing list of problems. The loss of land, harsh living conditions, and cultural upheaval left many Havasupai angry and demoralized.

Throughout much of the 20th century, the tribe waged a long-shot legal battle to reclaim much of their former territory. They were up against powerful forces. Their former territory belonged to Grand Canyon National Park, and both the park service and environmental organizations like the Sierra Club fought to keep the land in federal hands. The Havasupai, who had sustainably managed the land for centuries, were shocked when they were told to stay off the land so plants and animals could be protected.

Undeterred, the Havasupai continued to press their case. A turning point came in 1973, when Arizona Senator Barry Goldwater offered his support. Two years later, on January 4, 1975, over 250,000 acres were returned to the Havasupai tribe. In addition to land on the rim, the tribe regained control of the area below Havasu Falls, which had been operated as a national park campground. Seeking to alleviate the poverty that had plagued them for decades, the Havasupai took full control of Havasu Canyon's tourist operations.

Today tourism generates millions of dollars for the tribe. And though modernization has come to Supai in the form of electricity and mobile phones, the pace of life remains distinctly different. Suggestions to build a modern road into Havasu Canyon have always been rejected, and today the Havasupai boast the highest percentage of native speakers of any tribe in the U.S.

Wii Gl'iiva

These prominent rock spires, which guard the northern entrance to Havasu Canyon, are considered sacred by the Havasupai. Legend states that when the rocks fall, the walls of Havasu Canyon will close and the tribe will be no more.

Flooding in Havasu

Flooding is a fact of life in Havasu Canyon, which experiences a flood every three years on average. The canyon drains a watershed encompassing nearly 3,000 square miles, and runoff from thunderstorms funnels into Havasu Canyon with astonishing speed. Most floods are minor and merely a nuisance. But every few years a massive thunderstorm dumps enormous quantities of rain in a remarkably short period of time. Whenever this happens, the consequences for Havasu Canyon are severe.

In 1900 a woman named Flora Gregg Iliff was teaching in Havasu Canyon when she experienced a flash flood first-hand. Her terrifying account is recorded in her book *People of the Blue Water*: "With startling suddenness, a full-grown river, boiling with sand and debris, leaped over the east wall with a force that shot it far out into the canyon.... Nothing could stand against that roaring waterfall. It hurled a boulder over the rim, spun it crazily and smashed it on the ground with an impact that shook the canyon." During the flood, the Havasupai did what they have always done: retreat to high cliffs surrounding the canyon and wait for the waters to subside. The tribe always stored a year's worth of food in the cliffs above Supai in case flooding destroyed their crops.

In January 1910 the largest flood in recorded history tore through Havasu Canyon, peaking at an estimated 35,000 cubic feet per second (cfs)—1,000 times greater than Havasu Creek's normal flow. Every building in Supai was destroyed. Fortunately the flood occurred in winter, when most of the tribe was living on the rim, and many lives were spared. In 1990 the second-largest flood in recorded history tore through Havasu Canyon, peaking at roughly 20,000 cfs. Three years later, another flood maxed out at roughly 10,000 cfs. Flooding can occur in both winter and summer, but nearly 80 percent of historical Havasu Creek floods have occurred during or immediately following El Niño years.

More recently, in August 2008, a flash flood made headlines when it reshaped Havasu Canyon's famous waterfalls. The flood tore out a new streambed downstream of Supai, diverting the creek away from Navajo Falls (previously the first large waterfall below Supai) and creating two new waterfalls. Remarkably, the 2008 flood was estimated at only 6,000 cfs, making it the 17th-smallest flood in recorded history. But its power was severe. According to one witness in the campground, "All kinds of debris went rushing by including an outhouse, tents, water toys, cottonwood trees and boulders." Fortunately, thanks to the efforts of Havasupai first responders, there were no casualties in the campground and residents of Supai were unharmed. Search YouTube for "Havasu Flood 2008" to see dramatic video footage taken by visitors during the flood.

HAVASU CANYON

Beaver
Falls

Ukwalla
Point

Mooney
Falls

Havasu
Falls

Watahomigi
Point

Havasu Canyon

Manakacha
Point

Supai

Long Mesa

Hualapai Canyon

Hualapai
Hilltop

Supai Village

This small village, home to over 400 full-time residents, is the permanent home of the Havasupai Tribe. If you're arriving on foot, you'll reach Supai after twisting and turning through Havasu's narrow upper canyons. After descending into the large, open canyon floor, you'll follow a series of dusty dirt roads until you reach the tourist office, where all visitors must check in. Continue down the street to reach "downtown" Supai, home to the village cafe, market, post office, community center, and K-8 school. (When Havasupai children reach high school they attend a boarding school outside the canyon.) The Havasupai Lodge, a Christian church, and a Mormon church are also located nearby. Follow the main road north of the majestic *Wii Gl'iiva* and the road soon turns into a trail that heads down to Havasu Canyon's famous waterfalls and the campground.

Some visitors are dismayed by Supai. Hoping to experience a hidden paradise "uncorrupted" by the modern world, they encounter modest homes topped with satellite dishes and a helicopter dropping off supplies. The Havasupai are proud of their culture and continue to speak their native language, but they have embraced many aspects of the modern world. Some visitors are also surprised by the run-down condition of some parts of town. Remember that living in a remote, isolated canyon presents many challenges. You can't just run to the hardware store whenever something breaks. As you walk through Supai, remind yourself that you are a guest of the Havasupai and be respectful of their home.

Navajo Falls

The flash flood that tore through Havasu Canyon in August 2008 reshaped the scenery between Supai and Havasu Falls. The flood ripped out vegetation, carved out a new watercourse, and created two "new" waterfalls. In fact, prior to 1940, the uppermost waterfall existed and was called "Fifty-Foot Falls." A flash flood buried Fifty-Foot Falls in sediment, and it was re-exposed during the 2008 flood. Today, the upstream waterfall (right) is called Navajo Falls and the downstream waterfall (above) is called Little Navajo Falls. Navajo Falls is about 70 feet high, and Little Navajo Falls is about 30 feet high. Notice the vast stretch of dead trees on the ridge above Little Navajo Falls. Prior to 2008, Havasu Creek supported a riparian habitat along the ridge. Although the old habitat died after Havasu Creek shifted course, new habitat is slowly forming along the banks of the new route.

Havasu Creek's new waterway completely bypasses "Old" Navajo Falls, a 75-foot waterfall that was once considered one of Havasu Canyon's prettiest sights. It is frequently claimed that Old Navajo Falls was destroyed by the 2008 flood, but the waterfall's extensive travertine structure remains intact, creating, in effect, a "fossilized" waterfall. Although you can't see it from the trail, Old Navajo Falls is located downstream of Little Navajo Falls beyond the river's western bank. Although the loss of Old Navajo Falls is tragic, it's part of the natural cycle of destruction and regeneration that has shaped Havasu Canyon for thousands of years. And the "new" waterfalls sure are pretty.

Navajo Falls

Havasu Falls

Havasu Falls, the star attraction of Havasu Canyon, is located roughly half a mile past Navajo Falls. As the trail drops along the sheer western wall of Havasu Canyon, the roar of the falls grows louder. Suddenly, Havasu Falls appears on your right. At this point you're at eye level with the top of the 90-foot falls. Continue down the trail to reach several well-trodden side trails that lead to a beach area shaded by cottonwood trees. Although often crowded in summer, the beach is one of the most spectacular swimming holes in Arizona.

A century ago, Havasu Falls looked completely different. Back then the water tumbled over the cliff in a 200-foot-wide curtain of water called Bridal Veil Falls. In 1910 a flash flood roared through Havasu Canyon and knocked out a large notch in the cliff. In an instant, the water was channeled into a much narrower—and much more spectacular—waterfall. Other flash floods have been far less kind. In 1993 a flash flood destroyed several beautiful travertine terraces at the base of the waterfall that formed a series of cascading pools. Then, during the flood of 2008, the beautiful "apron" that defined the waterfall for decades was destroyed. The flood knocked out a small notch in the apron, creating a narrow chute that forms a far less dramatic waterfall. Take a look at the numerous travertine formations on either side of the falls. These are the prehistoric remnants of older versions of Havasu Falls. They are a useful reminder that, for thousands of years, the waterfall has naturally changed shape.

Why is the Water in Havasu Blue?

Even without its colorful, spring-fed creek, Havasu Canyon would be a remarkable destination. But the vibrant blue water, contrasted with striking red rocks, gives the canyon an otherworldly beauty. What makes the water so blue? The answer is chemistry—specifically, dissolved calcium carbonate and magnesium that occur naturally in Havasu Creek.

The process starts when rain falls on the surrounding plateaus and water seeps into the ground. Over thousands of years, the water slowly trickles through Grand Canyon's rock layers, dissolving rocks and picking up minerals along the way. Eventually the water reaches deep underground aquifers that feed Havasu Springs. (Carbon dating indicates that water flowing from Havasu Springs is over 11,000 years old). The water in Havasu Springs is saturated with calcium and bicarbonate (dissolved from limestone) and magnesium (which gives the water its brilliant blue tint). As the water enters the canyon, the sudden drop in pressure and increase in temperature causes solid calcium carbonate to precipitate out of the water. The calcium carbonate ultimately forms shiny layers of travertine along the creekbed, which further reflect the blue-tinted water. As the creek flows down the canyon, massive quantities of travertine are deposited—by some measures up to 70,000 pounds *each day*. This, in turn, leads to another fascinating phenomenon: as calcium bicarbonate precipitates out of the water, the relative saturation of magnesium increases. As a result, the water in Havasu Creek gets bluer and bluer the farther downstream it flows.

Mooney Falls

At 196 feet, Mooney Falls is the tallest waterfall in Havasu Canyon. To get there, follow the main trail one mile past Havasu Falls to a stunning overlook at the end of the campground. The path to the base of the falls is an Indiana Jones-style adventure that involves scrambling through a tunnel carved by 19th-century miners, followed by a slippery descent down a rickety ladder.

The Havasupai call this waterfall "Mother of the Waters." It is considered their most sacred waterfall. The name Mooney Falls comes from an unfortunate accident that occurred in 1880, when a group of American prospectors entered Havasu Canyon in search of gold. Their progress was halted when they reached the sheer cliffs surrounding the waterfall. A man named Daniel Mooney volunteered to be lowered down by rope, but on the way down his rope became stuck in a jagged crevice. As his friends struggled with the rope, it began to fray. Suddenly the rope snapped, and Mooney fell to his death. Unable to reach Mooney's body, the prospectors abandoned their search and went home. Ten months later they returned and built a ladder to the base of the falls. By that point Mooney's body had been encrusted in a fresh layer of travertine.

A few decades later, Mooney Falls was taken from the Havasupai tribe by the federal government. A private company attempted to build a hydroelectric plant in Havasu Canyon, but a flash flood tore through the canyon, destroying the machinery and bankrupting the company. In 1975 the government returned the waterfall to the Havasupai tribe.

Below Mooney Falls

Below Mooney Falls a rugged trail continues down Havasu Canyon all the way to the Colorado River. Along the way it passes through some of Havasu Canyon's most beautiful scenery. The water gets bluer. The vegetation gets lusher. And cascading pools are scattered between leafy expanses of wild grape. As you hike farther downstream, the crowds thin out. Soon it feels like you have Havasu Canyon all to yourself.

It's eight rugged miles from Mooney Falls to the Colorado River, which is beyond the limits of most day hikers. The most popular destination is Beaver Falls, located roughly four miles beyond the base of Mooney Falls at the conflux of Havasu Canyon and Beaver Canyon. Beaver Falls' cascading pools offer amazing scenery and divine swimming opportunities. In my opinion, it's one of the highlights of Havasu Canyon. But there's a catch. The trail below Mooney Falls is gorgeous, but it becomes harder to follow the farther downstream you go. A trip to Beaver Falls involves multiple river crossings and steep scrambles involving wobbly ladders and ropes. Experienced hikers with good route-finding skills can probably figure it out, but out-of-shape hikers uncomfortable with heights and river crossings should definitely avoid the long hike to Beaver Falls. If you've already made it to the base of Mooney Falls, however, it's definitely worth following the trail for as long as you feel comfortable. There's plenty of gorgeous scenery along the way.

Beaver Falls

Route 66

This 2,448-mile highway, completed in 1926, was the first major route between Chicago and Los Angeles. In the 1930s Route 66 served as the primary migration route for Dust Bowl refugees heading west. It was later made famous by the Bobby Troup song "(Get Your Kicks on) Route 66," which was covered by Nat King Cole, Perry Como, and Chuck Berry. Thanks to the song, Route 66 became a romantic symbol of American freedom. Following construction of the Interstate Highway System, however, Route 66 fell on hard times. As motorists abandoned the old two-lane highway for the speedier interstate, thousands of roadside mom-and-pop businesses closed down. By 1985 Route 66 was officially removed from the U.S. Highway System.

In recent years, however, Route 66 has experienced something of a revival. Although much of the original highway was swallowed up by Interstate 40, some classic stretches of Route 66 remain near Grand Canyon. Downtown Williams celebrates its Route 66 heritage through retro diners and coffee shops. But the most "authentic" experience lies 43 miles west in the town of Seligman. The real-life inspiration for the town of Radiator Springs in the Pixar movie *Cars*, Seligman is a shadow of its former self. Yet it still retains a charming, faded, 1950s-era vibe. Its most famous restaurant, Delgadillo's Snow Cap Drive-In, has been serving burgers, fries, and practical jokes since 1953. Past Seligman, Route 66 arcs northwest through the desert for 85 miles before rejoining with Interstate 40 in the town of Kingman.

Grand Canyon West

Owned and operated by the Hualapai tribe (p.76), Grand Canyon West encompasses 108 miles along Grand Canyon's southwest rim. Although not part of Grand Canyon National Park, its views are still breathtaking. Grand Canyon West is located 250 miles (5 hours driving) from Grand Canyon Village. From Las Vegas it's just 125 miles (2.5 hours driving), making it a popular destination for day-tripping tourists.

In addition to scenic viewpoints, Grand Canyon West offers horseback rides, helicopter tours, and rafting day trips along the Colorado River. Its most famous attraction, however, is the Grand Canyon Skywalk (above). This semi-circular bridge, which juts out 70 feet from Grand Canyon's rim, features a glass floor that offers visitors dramatic views 3,600 feet down to the Colorado River. When the Skywalk opened in 2007, astronaut Buzz Aldrin was the first person to walk across it publicly. He was followed by John Bennett Harrington, the first American Indian in space.

General admission to Grand Canyon West is $56 per person, which provides access to viewpoints, cultural activities, and live performances. Skywalk tickets are an additional $26 per person. Horseback tours, helicopter rides, and rafting trips require an additional fee. Overnight accommodations are available (888-868-9378, grandcanyonwest.com).

Extraordinary Guides to Extraordinary National Parks

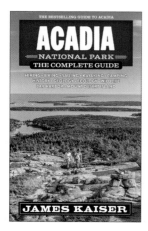

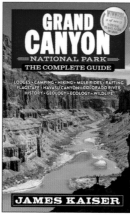

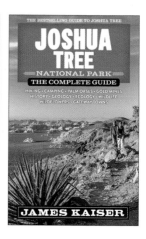

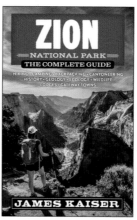

Need help customizing the perfect trip?

jameskaiser.com/travel-consulting